You are up to you.

YOU ARE UP TO YOU:
Innovate a new self for a new life, feel spiritually whole again after trauma and disability.

A NOTE TO THE READER Every effort has been made to ensure that the information contained in this book is complete and accurate. Names of individuals have been changed in all cases to protect the privacy of these persons. Neither the author nor publisher is engaged in rendering professional advice or services to the individual reader. The ideas, procedures, and suggestions contained in this book are not intended as a substitute for consulting with your physician or professional counselor. The advice and strategies contained herein may not be suitable for your situation. All matters regarding your health and wellbeing require medical supervision. Neither the author nor publisher shall be liable or responsible for any loss, injury, or damage allegedly arising from any information or suggestion in this book.

FIRST EDITION
Written, designed and illustrated by Ed Penniman

ISBN: 978-0-9974965-0-5 (softcover)

ISBN: 978-0-9974965-1-2 (e-book)

First Edition, October 2016

You are up to you.

Innovating a New Self for a New Life After Disability.
Feel spiritually whole again after trauma and disability.

Positive experiences from Guillain-Barré Syndrome.

BY ED PENNIMAN

This drawing of a happy little bee was carefully drawn with my mouth, the first piece of art after my quadriplegia.

—*EGP*

For those who have been given a huge challenge,
recognize an opportunity for personal growth and
are struggling to move forward with courage.

AUTHOR'S NOTE

I wrote this book because I want to share what I learned during my journey on the long path back to balance from loss, trauma and physical disability. I am one of the lucky ones. I was able to prevail over my challenge. To me, this means that I have done the deep work that allows me to live happily and appreciate what I have with authentic gratitude. During my difficult recovery back from total paralysis, I've discovered answers to many of the questions I faced as I struggled through the trauma of disability and evolved into what, I hope, is a more integrated being.

Much of my development after trauma came from doing my art, which gave me another way to express and learn about myself. I created all of the illustrations in this book. Most important among them are the self-portraits on the cover painted over several years representing my many different moods and characters. These images, some of several hundred self-portraits I've done, depict me in different guises and embrace the imperfect humanity of my face. By painting myself as a variety of characters, I created a way to literally face myself in all my varied aspects, Who are you really? When we are children we look up to certain people who represent qualities we find worthy and respectable. We are asked, "What do you want to be when you grow up?" We start with heroic figures, and with maturity we refine our vision of ourselves to align with our native talents and what ever gives us a sense of self-worth. I could have been any of the characters on the cover: a priest, cowboy, construction worker, banker, shaman, or others. But from the time we are children, we determine who we want to become, and we do it by choice.

This book is about not falling prey to a negative self-concept after trauma. It is about redefining how you see yourself, how to take your personal challenge and learn the valuable embedded lesson it may offer. I evolved as a person because I was made aware that I could be a better me after being stripped of my limited ideas of myself. I was given an opportunity to renew and rebrand myself – to live from a deeper and evolving image of who I am.

ACKNOWLEDGEMENTS

I would like to thank those who encouraged me to continue with what I have referred to as my writing project. I'm glad I was told by therapists to keep notes in journals of my experiences and feelings. My past notes have helped flesh out important content and detail. I especially appreciate the insight, intellect and key suggestions of Michael Ray, Ph.D. who served as a seasoned scout on my spiritual writing path. Also, those who showed sincere interest, read drafts, and contributed ideas to organize and prune content. I appreciate the inspiration, editing, love, encouragement, conversation, motivation and support of Anna May Churchill Guagnini, Carol Pista, Cindy Ranii, Neil Brown LCSW, Marilyn Churchill, Philip J. Wagner, Manfred, Nancy Manos RN, Oksana Chabanenko, TMike Walker, Edward Frost and a very sincere thank you to Coralie Hunter for her insightful structural editing and astute suggestions. Most importantly I want to acknowledge GBS/CIDP Foundation International founders Estelle and Robert Benson for their dedication to provide education, research, support and assistance to benefit Guillain-Barré/Chronic Inflammatory Demylinating Polyneuropathy patients and their families.

CONTENTS

INTRODUCTION:

There's no silver bullet.

When I became disabled as a quadriplegic, it was a devastating change for me. I was 42 and my life's path took an abrupt turn into uncharted, painful-to-navigate physical, emotional, psychological and spiritual territories.

I felt the shock most initially when I went into convulsions and was admitted to the Emergency Room. I had no idea what was happening in my body. I was smart and aware enough to read the faces and energy of the attending physicians. I was an out of the ordinary admittance. When I was diagnosed with GBS, I felt my life spin out of my control. Fear was at the forefront of everything. I didn't know if I would recover from my paralysis and lead a normal active life ever again.

Guillain-Barré syndrome (GBS) is a rare disorder in which a person's own immune system damages their nerve cells, causing muscle weakness and paralysis. GBS can cause symptoms that last for a few weeks. Most people recover fully from GBS, but some people have permanent nerve damage. In very rare cases, people have died of GBS, usually from difficulty breathing. In the United States, for example, an estimated 3,000 to 6,000 people develop GBS each year.

Many things can cause GBS. About two-thirds of people who develop GBS symptoms do so several days or weeks after they have been sick with diarrhea or a respiratory illness. Infection with the bacterium Campylobacter jejuni is one of the most common risk factors for GBS. Most cases of Campylobacter jejuni come from handling or ingesting raw or undercooked poultry meat. Although poultry and other birds are not affected by the bacterium, other animals can be. Therefore it is possible for a person to acquire the infection from contact with infected stool of an ill cat or dog. People also can develop GBS after having the flu or other infections, such as cytomegalovirus and Epstein Barr virus. On very rare occasions, they may develop GBS in the days or weeks after getting a vaccination.

Though it was too soon to guess at what the future might hold for me, I knew I had to overcome my fear of being a quadriplegic in the present. This experience was a monumental change for me on all levels of my life experience. I had degenerated from a highly functioning manager into a devastated dependant being reliant on others for my every need. I decided that a positive attitude would be a better mental environment for any fears I had about something that I could not control. My positive attitude served me well and provided me with hope – a hope that I would be OK. I had heard reports at both ends of the Guillain–Barré Syndrome prognosis spectrum. Some patients simply got better, some died, and others were in a variety of degrees of healing. Some played golf again; some were in a wheelchair forever. All I could really do was to rise above my fear and be hopeful.

Your growth, healing and recovery depend on you, and you alone. If you can find someone who loves you, whether a family member or a friend, it will help you along your path. It has been over thirty years since I was stricken by Guillain-Barré Syndrome, and I have learned that it is up to me to make the best of my situation. I will never be the same as I was before, and, frankly, I like the new me a whole lot better. My experience helped me to slow down, look at myself, stop comparing myself to others and really reinvent myself from scratch. I believe that this was an opportunity for me to become compassionate and find more authentic experiences in my life, experiences that would have been lost to the former me. I would say that if you are reading this book, you are on your way to achieving the right mind-set for emotional healing. Also, if you have a loved one who is being challenged and is lucky enough to have you as a partner, then you can use these ideas to help them along their path of physical recuperation and regeneration of spirit and mind.

One of my most treasured gems of personal growth was that of developing a "witness consciousness." It has allowed me the wisdom and grace to engage pain at a level that would have been impossible for me before my journey into my better self. This consciousness was born by my near death experience. When I found myself looking down on my physical body lying on the hospital bed, I became clearly aware of the separation of my mind and my body. This insight revealed how I could view myself from a higher plane. The witness consciousness provides us with a way to see ourselves objectively in context, and brings to the situation rationality, distance, and balance. This gives us an opportunity to be non-reactionary and wise. My trauma made me a better, more lovable man. This disease happened to me by accident, there is no blame, no defining moment, no fickle finger of fate that transformed me into the "other" on life's stage. I have let go of riding my bike in the spring mountain air, playing beach volleyball with tanned and fit buddies, and carrying my lover to our bed for lovemaking, and I count it as a blessing that I did not die.

After I was physically able to write again, I started to keep personal journals about my feelings and experiences. It was a way for me to share my feelings and insights with my later self. It was a place I could go to say anything I wanted to without fear of misunderstanding or reprisal. In many ways it was a good way to download feelings without any systematic obligation; I did it for no reason other than that of free self-expression. Occasionally I would go back and read some pages that reminded me of a present entry I was making. It was then that I discovered my personal behavioral patterns.

One New Year's Eve I had several invitations to join friends to hail in the New Year, but I declined. I decided to have a more conscious, introspective version of the celebration. It was a time to celebrate the blessings, tests and lessons of the previous year as well as the potential for success and happiness in the next. I wanted to celebrate consciously, through the night and into the next day. That year my celebration was a solo flight, and I went to bed at three in the morning.

This writing is a window into the many insights, years of journal entries, personal growth and that New Year's evening that I chose to spend by myself rather than with friends. I was faced with two things that were changing and challenging me. I had recently self published my poetry book, *In Memoriam Innocentium*, a collection of prose and poetry about love, loss, disability, spiritual healing, and accepting the dissolution and finalization of my third marriage. It was time for me to take a really good look at myself in the mirror. As you read this book perhaps you can do the same and take a few ideas with you that will become tools to rebuild your personal joy and start to honor yourself again, or perhaps for the first time.

Whether you are sitting alone now in an empty home recently vacated by your beloved, or lying on your back at the dawn of a new life situation after an accident or disease, or simply wondering what to do with your unfulfilled self, I believe that there are some things I can share with you. I'd like to help you find some clarity and peace of mind ... maybe even happiness. I am not saying that I have it completely together, but I do have enough clarity to see others struggling with some of the same challenges I have prevailed over. Be it karma, cosmic chaos, optimistic innocence or the ultimate fruits of selfishness or dishonesty, these lessons have been experienced, studied and learned by me. Though there are days when I come close to making some of the same old mistakes, I am able to catch myself at the first untaken step toward self-generated pain and unhappiness.

As a disabled person, I naturally use references to physical disability and trauma. Trauma includes the death of a loved one, divorce, physical loss, or any type of life changing event that is irrevocable. You can easily substitute the words of your choice for disabled and this information will work for you because this book is about loss, reorientation and recovery.

I hope that this book can help you journey forward with awareness and appreciation of who you are, can be, and how you can bring this into the world.

Chapter 1

CAPTAIN AHAB BECKONS:

My story.

Faith is the bird that feels the light when the dawn is still dark.
–Rabindranath Tagore

I was born in 1942 in the small coastal town of Santa Cruz, California and grew up there with two brothers and a sister. I am the artist in the family. I had loving and special people for parents and enjoyed a good upbringing. My father was raised as a Christian Scientist and my mother as a Catholic. I believe I benefited from the best and worst of both. I have always had an awareness of God in my life and, like some people, the degree of my religious involvement depended upon my struggle at hand. My grandparents were productive and well respected. I went to Santa Cruz High School, Cabrillo College, then moved to Los Angeles where I attended Chouinard Art School at the California Institute of the Arts, where I earned a Bachelor of Fine Art in Advertising Design, specializing in Marketing Communications.

After graduating, I established myself quickly in the design world, garnering many design awards for my work.

But when I started my own business in the 70's, it turned out that the Santa Cruz market could not support my company and me. I had an elegant office on what was then called the Pacific Garden Mall, it was the heart of Santa Cruz in the 70's, a brilliant and creative time. But some clients didn't pay me and it took a heavy toll. I should have moved my office to Palo Alto, but I was overly optimistic, thinking my design awards would bring more business to me. They did not. I was tired of feeling low because of money problems.

I closed my office and decided to go into my family's land title insurance and escrow business. It was disheartening as I started at a low-base pay, but by then I had two small sons to take care of, David and Ian, so I appreciated the steady paycheck. My older brother, Warren Junior, had worked for the family business since high school and resented me working in what he felt was his domain. Looking back now I cannot blame him. I learned to be an escrow secretary, an escrow officer and had a knack for marketing the services. But essentially I was still financially "paralyzed", even though I had made a positive difference in terms of increasing the volume of business. I received several raises over time, but I believed my efforts and accomplishments were misunderstood and minimized.

I had been frustrated in my design business, but in retrospect I now see that I jumped from a financial frying pan into a psychic fire. I was working for my family – the key word being "for" – when I should have been working "with" them. I had become stifled; I was a mental time bomb waiting to explode and I didn't know it. I felt that because I was not privy to the net financial benefits of the business, that I was not really part of the family.

To make matters worse, my marriage was in serious trouble. My first wife brought distrust into our marriage from a previous relationship with a boyfriend who had cheated on her. She saw everything I chose to do and my outgoing personality through a filter of distrust, skepticism and jealousy. For my part, I had allowed my own selfishness and frustration to come between us. The marriage had disintegrated to the level of her deciding that I was someone who could not be trusted and, from her standpoint, was always wrong. I developed a good case of passive aggressiveness and soon the relationship was doomed. I had come from a family with a very strong matriarchal core and had vowed personally never to allow myself to become emasculated.

It was around this time that I met my second wife, Sandra "Susie" at a photo-shoot where she was modeling. She had it all, plus I could talk to her without her judgment. We had a lot of fun together, even though I was still married at the time, which added to the excitement and the challenge. It was not a good situation at all. I was hooked, and so was she because we were really good together. Susie encouraged me to work in Silicon Valley. I left my first wife, left my job with the family business, and then I left town. I believe there was a deep chasm between my sense of self-awareness and self-respect then. Nevertheless, I got great job offers from Hewlett-Packard and National Semiconductor Corporation in their Marketing Communications Departments. National's job description was a better fit and offered more compensation.

By quitting the family business and moving into the corporate world where I was judged solely on my merits, I more than doubled my salary and benefits. I took the position at National Semiconductor Corporation in Santa Clara, California, as the Graphics Manager.

Suddenly my whole life shifted. Although I had tried hard at the family business, the financial remuneration was not adequate. At my new job in Silicon Valley I was a star, respected, valued, and I earned more money than ever before in my life. With four assistant managers and 12 graphic designers in my department who had respect for me and worked hard for me, I had all I needed to repair my self-respect, which had been so damaged in my previous job and marriage. It was a powerful position and a heady experience. I was remarried to a sexy, beautiful, fun and supportive woman, had a new five-bedroom custom home in the Soquel hills of Santa

Cruz County and two smart and pretty stepdaughters. Susie was a real estate agent and helped financially, but it didn't matter what she earned as I made enough to easily support it all, the power was intoxicating. I did freelance design work for National Advanced Systems, a National subsidiary, adding to the income.

This was the early 80's and work was thrilling. Money for design projects was seemingly unlimited— with my department budget in the millions of dollars. The women at work wanted a piece of my magic and let me know it. I was not available and I let them know, but I did flirt with them. My income was flowing and I had my eye on a new Porsche Turbo Carrera. It was metallic chocolate colored with natural leather interior. The car was a statement about my new "successful" life. It was fast, expensive, stylish and pretentious...perfect for me. I had no awareness of what was happening to me. I was becoming mindlessly self-centered. My former wife was struggling financially and my sons were getting into trouble at school and with the authorities. I deeply regret that I was indifferent to my own sons at this time. But it was all about me as I played the role of a big shot at work, I was a good fit and my creative contributions noteworthy. I had become a kind of celebrity and dressed the part. I was tall, dark and handsome, and had plenty of cash. My ego was getting a real "fix", but I was spiritually asleep.

In short, the swing of the financial and self-centered pendulum had reached its farthest point in the arc, and all seemed to be going my way.

I was living my life the way I wanted to, not the way I thought I should morally. There is no harsh self-judgment here, but an honest, self-appraisal based on what my true moral values were and how I was raised. I had started to make decisions based solely on what was going to maximize my pleasure in life.

An Omen from the Future.

On a Monday morning I left for work at 6:45, which would put me in Santa Clara at 8 a.m. As I drove down the hill from home, I noticed a disabled person who had fallen and become entangled in a patch of ivy. I had a clear view of him as he frantically waved at me to help him get up and untangle him from his snare. I looked at him indifferently and drove on. My thought was that I was sure someone else would come along at any moment and they could rescue him, plus I was wearing a new Italian suit and expensive Italian shoes that I didn't want to get dirty or scuffed up. In short, I chose to do nothing.

The image of his face looking at me imploringly with his free hand beckoning to me is burned into my mind to this day. It kept appearing and reappearing during my commute and distracted me at work. I started to think about how little time and effort it would have cost me to stop and extricate him. The image reminded me of the scene in the film *Moby Dick* where Captain Ahab had finally harpooned the great white whale. Ahab had been pulled into the sea by the harpoon line which had trapped him against the body of the whale as it dived deeply into the water. As the whale re-surfaced, dead Ahab's one free arm could be seen repeatedly flapping back and forth as if to beckon for help.

On some deep level I had been traumatized by betraying my own basic humanity when I deliberately failed to help that man. The image of that young disabled fellow returned time and again that night and more again into the next day. A few days later I came down with a bad cold. I had no idea that just a few days later I would be completely paralyzed.

On the morning of March 1, 1984, I was due to fly to Los Angeles to review concepts for the National Semiconductor Corporation's annual report. At about 3 a.m., I woke up because I needed to go to the bathroom. I was sleeping comfortably without any forewarning of physical problems. But when I got out of bed I noticed I was very dizzy. I returned to bed and slept until my alarm went off at 6 a.m. As I attempted to get up, the dizziness increased three fold, and I could not stand without assistance. I noticed that rather than being energetic I felt my energy sapped. Something was wrong. I thought I must have been having a mild relapse of the flu. I asked Susie to please call my doctor's office and she made an appointment for 11.

We discovered I was too weak even to dress myself and my lack of balance was now accompanied by disorientation. As Susie dressed me, I got my first wave of fear. I had never felt like that before. The closest feeling was like being spun around and around until I was staggeringly dizzy. The world was spinning all around me as I tried to walk, then there was nausea and more fear. She and I lay on the bed and waited for the appointment time. When I started to feel worse we decided that we should eat and then go to the Emergency Room. As I attempted to go upstairs from the master bedroom to the kitchen I went into convulsions. I fell to the floor and struck my head on the wall on the way down. I remember feeling the cold marble of the entryway floor on my back as I began to lose consciousness. Susie called 911 and the paramedics arrived shortly. I don't recall the trip to the ER. I was already in trauma and slipping in and out of consciousness.

The attending ER physician immediately commenced the process of diagnosis with a complete blood panel. I remember a tingling feeling in my right toes. This was the beginning of a long, painful and arduous journey. I would never be the same after that morning.

Symptoms of Guillain-Barré Syndrome are first noticed as numbness, tingling, pain and weakness. I had all the initial symptoms. At first this is usually in the toes and feet, eventually moving up the body as an ascending paralysis. I felt this bilaterally with accompanying numbness mostly in my lower extremities, but the local neurologists did not initially or speedily confirm the diagnosis of Guillain-Barré Syndrome.

The experience of these first symptoms was extreme. I felt I was being helplessly carried on a piece of wreckage of myself. Time flowed painfully slow that morning, and by the afternoon, I had lost my ability to lift my arms off the bed. My feelings ranged from panic and fear to a deep sense of dread and disappointment. Even though I was supposed to be in Los Angeles on business, and to direct the most important project I had worked on to date, I didn't care. My job had suddenly become insignificant. I was caught up in a new, foreign culture of sterility, attending physicians, medical staff, monitoring devices and the jarring cacophony of hospital sounds.

My wife was strong and confident during this process. She was stepping up and doing all she could to allay my fears when she had deep dread of her own. She didn't leave my side for a minute during the whole ordeal. It was an example of one giving from a place of love and generosity in the most dire of times. I could see it was breaking her heart to see me suffering.

For myself and Susie, I tried to move but I couldn't. The experience was like twilight sleep when one is half awake, trying to move or yell but the body doesn't respond. This disconnect was now my waking reality. I wanted to move, the signals were attempting to go from my brain to my muscles, but nothing was happening. The disease had destroyed my motor nerves and no neurological signals were connecting. For the first time in my life my body was inert, involuntarily grounded by forces of gravity now stronger than me.

To make matters worse, I was not getting any information from the neurologists who had come to examine and test me. They tested my reflexes, did a sharp point test, and ran a little wheel with pinpoints on it to determine if I could feel. This was a test that I would undergo many times in the months ahead.

I didn't know enough about my condition to have rational thoughts about what was happening to me. I learned that the doctors felt the same way; they were mystified about my condition. The attending neurologist said they couldn't learn any more about my illness until they performed a spinal tap. The fact that the doctors did not know what was wrong gave me a jolt of fear that served to push my hope and spirit down even lower than it already had been. It was in that moment that my wife Susie and I realized I was fighting for my life.

Instead, the neurologist told me the problem was in my spine. In a fetal position I felt a large spinal tap needle penetrate deeply into my back. Then after waiting for hours for an analysis of the spinal fluid, the neurologist was not sure enough to make a solid diagnosis. When he initially said "spine," I had a deep sinking feeling that I was involved in a mortal struggle. Fear struck me in the heart like never before. During this acute destructive neurological phase I was given periodic tests with a spirometer to determine the function of my lungs. This was called a PFT or pulmonary function test. It measured the volume and speed of air inhaled and exhaled. As the various tests were given to me they revealed how seriously ill I was.

My emotional and psychological state was tested as well. The greatest concern then was that if I lost lung function, I would be a candidate for a tracheotomy. If my lungs failed they would cut a hole in my windpipe and put me on a ventilator. I passed the PFT— I learned that I had a grand lung capacity from diving, swimming and playing the trombone for many years. I was extremely relieved to not have to endure choking, suction treatments and everything else connected with a tracheotomy. I didn't know it, but my wife Susie was told to get the family in to see me within 48 hours, essentially to say goodbye. The priest at the hospital gave me the "Sacrament of the Sick" or the "Last Rights." This sacrament is administered both to the dying and to those who are gravely ill or are about to undergo a serious operation, for the recovery of their health and for spiritual strength.

After only three days in the hospital, I was completely paralyzed, had lost bladder and bowel control, and could only slightly move my head. Later I was fitted with a blowpipe so that when I blew on it a light would come on at the nurses' station. By this time the pain in my head had increased the point where my eyes ached and my head felt like it was splitting open. My back felt like I had a hatchet buried in my spine from which a searing pain migrated up and down. The lack of motion caused sharp, painful pinpricks over my entire body. My limbs became hypersensitive, and I would cry out if I were touched anywhere but on my joints. In order to lessen my pain, Susie and the nurses would move my body and give me range of motion treatments. This was done for three days and nights continuously. I had to be turned every two hours so the weight of my body wouldn't break down my skin. I wanted so badly to move on my own but couldn't. My wife was dedicated to me through my ordeal and she proved her love for me over and over.

I tried to cover up my pain and fear with humor—an act of survival. What I was really thinking was how could this have happened to me. The degree of the unknown at that time compared to today was great. Information was not readily available on the Internet and there was no Wikipedia. Deep down I was feeling the darkness of extinction. My awareness level was as acute as it could be, and I easily read the worrisome facial expressions and body language of those around me. Every sense I had became sharper as I teetered on the precarious edge of my life. I was scared to death and my way to do my part for those loved ones who were suffering with me was to lighten the situation with humor where I could find it. It was a type of cynical, witless and fatalistic humor. As I languished in the hospital ER, it was hard to take anything seriously, because I could see my own death. There was nothing funny about being ravaged by this disease. I knew it, and my family knew it.

I remained in this dreadful state without a definitive diagnosis for two weeks. Finally, I was tentatively diagnosed as having both post-infectious encephalomyelitis and Guillain-Barré syndrome. My two neurologists could not agree on which one it was.

A PAINFUL REBIRTH.

I was told that there was nothing more they could do for me at the Dominican Hospital in Santa Cruz, so, at the urging of my then brother-in-law, Ronald Dunton, I was admitted to University of California Hospital in San Francisco. There I underwent a series of blood purification treatments. The idea behind this then new treatment was simple: instead of trying to suppress the immune system with powerful medication alone, auto-antibodies were mechanically removed from my blood during a process similar to dialysis treatment. The procedure later became known as plasmapheresis, or plasma separation and plasma exchange.

At night in my hospital bed, after hours of plasma exchange treatment, I felt a peaceful yet odd sensation I had never experienced before. I first realized it when I felt and sensed myself looking down at myself in my hospital bed. I felt myself in and out of my body at the same time. There were two parts of me that were being drawn subtly apart. I can only describe the feeling as something like looking through an old-fashioned single lens reflex camera, when the image in the lens is divided so that one may adjust the lens and bring the image into focus. I realized later that I was having an inner dialog with myself. I was deciding whether to let my mind and body separate or to bring the strange sense of duality I was experiencing back into focus. It may have been a dream, but I don't think so because it was so very powerful. For the first time in my life it allowed me to sense a real defining line between the physical and spiritual worlds. This near-death experience revealed to me the duality of my being and birthed my witness consciousness.

At that time I didn't know if I was going to live or die. I hadn't eaten in over a week; I couldn't swallow. I had lost weight and was going slightly mad. As I was lying in the hospital bed I could hear the cries of other patients' praying, groaning and the general madness in the hospital throughout the nights. Day after day I would grow more accustomed to the rhythm of the hospital. I learned the codes for various emergencies and for patients who had died. I had family members and friends visit me. Also, an outreach group ministered to my spiritual needs and many people came in to pray for me. What I was struck by the most was the confidence of people who were trusting in God that I would be OK. My brother Mark, a spiritual man, made audio tapes for me, he read from his Bible, and selected verses that had been a help to him.

ON TO REHAB AND MY FUTURE

After about a month, I had lost more than 50 pounds, I couldn't sleep at night and only catnapped during the day. I was hyper-sensitive to everything. The smallest itch I could not scratch would become a consuming, burrowing pain. I decided to try to deal with the pain by disassociating myself from it.

I was transferred from UCSF Hospital to Ralph K. Davies, a rehabilitation hospital in San Francisco where I would stay for five months. I tried to have faith, be patient and hopeful. I prayed as each day crawled by slowly. There were times it seemed as if the clock had stopped running. But I seriously worked at my therapy. During the time at the rehab hospital, I had a group of Christian brothers lay their hands on me for a healing.

The power of their prayers and the faith they displayed convinced me that soon I would just get right up out of bed and head for home. I was wrong. Nothing happened. I lay there paralyzed, unable to move anything. After months, I could only shrug a shoulder slightly.

It takes time to heal, and sometimes if the healing doesn't happen as hoped, we are left scarred or disfigured. In my case, my legs and arms and intrinsic hand muscles are permanently atrophied due to neurological damage. On one level, I am angry about it, but perhaps on a deeper level I am just grateful it is not worse.

I was angry that the disease happened to me and there was no logical or rational reason why. I was told what might have caused it, but it was all supposition. I found that the path of anger I was going down was much like the path of jealousy. The feelings and thoughts seemed to feed on themselves leading to more and more intense emotions.

Paying attention to what triggered my anger eventually helped me cope. There was a feeling of injustice that this happened to me. I was a good guy, why couldn't this have happened to a lesser person? I wondered if there were acts I had committed to deserve this? I didn't think so, I still don't. The damage was done to my nerves and it was a done deal. I may or may not get better, time would tell. I had sadness and if I dwelled on the injustice of it I would get angry.

I was often frustrated particularly when I realized how dependent I was on others for so many aspects of my life. For example I needed to be turned in my hospital bed so that I wouldn't get bedsores. I appreciated the help and I think this kept my anger at bay. Frustration was going to be a big part of my life now and I had to adapt to it. Anger and frustration a can lead to aggressive behavior. This is usually expressed in a safe zone with loved ones. This can destroy relationships. I saw this acted out over and over again by patients and I swore to myself I would never be like that.

If we can be heads up enough to sit with and understand the root cause of our feelings before expressing them then we can manage anger. We can harness anger to try harder and to develop patience.

When I compare myself now to where I was in the acute phase and early on in my rehabilitation, I am better and that is positive and a good thing. I learned that if I compared myself to what I was like before the onset of my disease that it was foolish and a recipe for emotional destruction.

I was so shocked with the suddenness of my situation it was hard to believe. But, like anything else, an enduring life situation cannot help but display ones new reality. At various stages of recovery you will stop and have a reality check and perceive yourself objectively. That is the time to get basic with yourself and appreciate your improved situation no matter how small and incremental. I learned patience this way, with my lot in life, with myself and with those around me.

I think a small amount of denial is OK. It is natural to start thinking this way but it is so dangerous to our self. It can destroy our openness to experience and the good that may come to us through this tribulation. Denial will rob us of hope and hope is everything. Don't extinguish your hope but maintain your positive mind-set. The fact you may be yearning for a miracle is not a bad thing, that is just an expression of hope and it is natural. It helps us move forward and balanced in our task of this healing episode. If you decide to dwell in denial, your payoff will be negative physical and psychological symptoms like fatigue, headaches, digestive and internal problems. I can say that because I experienced this when I was in denial. This does not embarrass me as I learned it is an incremental and healthy step to healing and acceptance. Prevailing over denial will yield you the gift of independence and decisiveness. Be open to the endowment you have been given, as it will define the difference between being handicapped by your experience or propelled to a higher level of consciousness and self-acceptance. You will always have potential, and denial robs you of that. Sometimes at night when I look at my hands I still can't believe that this has happened to me, but I accept it.

My mind drifted back to that morning so long ago when I turned an indifferent eye to a disabled man who had fallen down. I see him waving to me, and, as I do, I see and feel myself in his position after falling. That man was me. I just didn't realize it at the time.

Chapter 2

YOU ARE UP TO YOU:
Coming to Grips with Vulnerability

The marvelous richness of human experience would lose something
of rewarding joy if there were no limitations to overcome.
—Helen Keller

The past, the present and the future — these are all things I had a lot
of time to think about when I was in the hospital. It took me a few
weeks until what was happening to me started to sink in. There was so
much activity surrounding me in the hospital that I got caught up in being
a patient, rather than being myself. I slowly started to understand that I
was a quadriplegic. Realizing my situation or owning it would take time. In
this new life, I had become used to being dictated to by various physicians.
They announced what would be happening to me, and I accepted what I
was told because I had no experience or power. I did have family, but they
were, of course, as much caught up in the medical process as I was.

Owning one's disability goes beyond physiological limitations. The
physical challenge begins to dissolve one's identity or self-concept by one
unpleasant experience after the other. I knew I had to be fed, turned in my
hospital bed every two hours, given range-of-motion treatments, bathed
with a sponge, and moved from place to place as needed, depending upon
what the next doctor's order was. But certain things really drove my new
reality home. They say little things mean a lot. I never realized how often,
as humans, we need to scratch an itch. It is constant, I would challenge
you to not scratch your next itch and see what it feels like. Don't give in
to it just sit with the itch. You will experience for the first time in your life

what it feels like to not be able to satisfy the simplest of needs. The itch will become the focal point of your mind and cause you to become agitated. If you have had the misfortune to have a broken arm in a solid cast, you will have experienced the similar unpleasant experience of not being able to reach in and satisfy the itch inside the cast.

I also felt and experienced for the first time the sheer gravity and the dead weight of my limp body pressing against the hospital bed or onto the gurney when transferred. Finding myself immobile and at the mercy of staff to safely transport me, I owned the full impact of what quadriplegia was. I didn't know it then, but I was about to experience what it's like to lie flat for months at a time, with only a slight elevation during feeding time. My world had suddenly been constricted. I was now limited to a small hospital room shared with another acutely ill patient. I went from living in my comfortable home in the hills, and driving a BMW over the beautiful Santa Cruz Mountains each day to the expansive campus of National Semiconductor's world headquarters, to the shocking and unexpected limitations of hospital living.

I was like a high-flying bird winging my way forward then suddenly shot and falling helplessly to the earth. I was lying on the ground, damaged and vulnerable. The situation I was in was worse than being imprisoned. It is one thing to be segregated from others, but quite another to be fractured from your self. It is another layer of isolation that yields the experiential distinction of mind-body separation. In this state I was just my thoughts and what was left of my functioning body. It was a time for me to realize that I must pick up what was left of myself and go bravely forward.

There was a period of what might be called "scab picking." I enjoyed the fantasy of going back in my mind to riding my bike, meeting my buddies to play beach volleyball, and other physical activities. Eventually, however, I realized that fantasizing did no good. I was beginning to try to let go of all that, but I couldn't. I was never a jock, but one does not have to be one to enjoy normal physical pleasures. I had to start putting physical recollections out of my mind that would be momentarily pleasurable, because I would find myself saddened to the point of depression. I was angry and feeling sorry for myself all the time.

COMING TO GRIPS WITH TOTAL VULNERABILITY.

During this early, critical phase of my disease, right after I had been transferred to the Ralph K. Davies rehab facility at Franklin Hospital, I had an eye-opening encounter with another patient. I don't remember the patient's name but I learned that he was a dentist; he was gay and had a gay clientele. The AIDS epidemic was running rampant in the gay community in the early 80's in San Francisco. Fear of AIDS was at its height as there were still so many unanswered questions about how the disease was contracted. At the time, it was called the "gay disease." There was a growing resentment of gays that led to isolation and consolidation of the gay community in one area of San Francisco. As part of the AIDS scare, it became hard for gay men to get medical attention including medical services like dentistry. The gay community stuck together and helped one another. It was a time when communal compassion outpaced fear of AIDS. At some point this dentist had contracted herpes which had infected his brain. He was in rehab, recovering from a brain surgery that resulted in the removal of a large part of his brain. His head was terribly caved in on one side. He was often very agitated, strapped to his bed, on monitors and IVs.

Often patients were shifted around and our hospital rooms were traded. This happened from time to time to maintain harmony within the patient community. I was moved into the room that used to belong to the dentist, and he was moved to another room just down the hall. I was still a complete quadriplegic and was set up to call the nursing station by pressing my cheek against what was called a "pancake," a flat air-filled bag that would trigger a nurse call button when compressed.

I had developed a case of "sundowner's syndrome" as had most of the patients who were not overmedicated. This syndrome is a survival tactic during the long nights when the hospital is understaffed. One can only sleep during the day when there is enough staff around to feel safe. It was about 3:30 in the morning when the door to my room opened, and the dentist entered in a frenzied state. He had broken out of his restraints, pulled out his IVs. Blood was running down his arms and neck. He came over to me, as I lay paralyzed in my hospital bed, and hovering over me he said, "You are in my room. What have you done with all my things? You are a bad person!" He came closer to my face now and with a crazy look in his eye he repeated, "Why are you in my room, this is mine, where are my things … look. Nothing of mine is in here, where are they, what have you done with them?"

From the moment he entered my room, I started pressing the pancake with my cheek. It was in the middle of the night, the staff was sparse and those on the night shift, I thought, were a bunch of odd ducks that didn't seem to pay much attention to the needs of patients. To be fair there were some fine night nurses. But in general, when a patient called, the nurses would usually finish their conversation before attending to the patient's needs.

After what seemed like an hour, I am sure it wasn't, a nurse entered my hospital room and took control of the situation. The male nurse guided the dentist with assurance and compassion back to the correct room. I am not sure what happened to the dentist, but he was removed from the rehab hospital after that incident.

This experience was the closest to madness and possible extinction I have ever experienced. In that brief moment, I was confronted with my mortality. Alone and desolate, I realized how absolutely vulnerable I was. To this day I am not sure how much danger I was in. I do know he didn't make contact with me, the staff cleaned up the blood from the floor and all was set straight. But I was completely unprotected in that situation. I was not prepared in any way for the danger of being completely helpless. It was extremely traumatic for me, and I had to seek counseling with the staff psychiatrist. I had learned at the deepest and most profound level how absolutely vulnerable I was, being quadriplegic.

GROW IN AND BEYOND THE PRESENT UGLY MOMENT.

At this critical juncture I realized that I had to first and foremost own that I always had a choice when it comes to how I feel about, and deal with, being placed on a new path. I would get discouraged at times, but chose to believe that in God's good time all things would work out for the best. I was not ready to die. God had a plan for me and maybe my atrophied body was a part of it. Adapting to and growing from my trauma was the biggest, hardest, most all-encompassing work I would ever do. It is lonely and singular, like a spiritual retreat or a prison term. But it was time to stop and consider all that was behind and before me.

I knew in that moment when the dentist entered my room that I had to get past the loss of function in my body; I had to regain some control. I couldn't have a ritual burial of my arms and legs as they were still very much there, as well as the prospect of full neurological and muscular recovery. What I did have to bury, and consciously so, was my tendency to "check out" into a dream reverie of past physical enjoyments. I did this by staying in the ugly present moment. I found that getting into the present moment served to put a "period" at the end of a destructive behavior that only served to connect me with the past and emotionally cushion me from the hard work of dealing with my present and future traumatic reality.

I had been given a good prognosis for a full recovery. This is often the case with GBS, because there is really no way to tell how much one will

be affected after the disease has run its course. So, while I didn't know if I would ever regain movement in my arms and legs, perhaps my good prognosis had a placebo effect that pulled me forward, or pulls others forward for that matter. I do know the placebo effect is a strong one that can lead to better health. The power of the mind as it relates to healing is a very strong force, which has yet to be fully comprehended.

There is security in the known. It may be that the known, or a definitive prognosis, is the archenemy of positive healing. It can rob us of hope, or it may exterminate faith in our healing. The distance is uncomfortable between what we have (where we are in the healing process) and what we need and want for our healthy growth and recovery. My situation was completely unknown. Though I did not have control of my body, I did have control of my mind though there were times I thought I may be losing it. Still, I knew I had no choice but to prevail over my situation. In retrospect, I am glad the prognosis was positive and my situation ambiguous; it left a lot of room for hope and positive thinking.

The reason people are in awe of survivors is because survivors have dug deeper into themselves than they ever knew they could, pulled up the fortitude residing in the depths of their being and prevailed in their challenge to live a full and meaningful life. Is it possible to have victory emotionally without the probability of prevailing over your disability? Yes.

When I say prevail over disability, I mean live in full acceptance, not dwelling in wishful thinking that damaged nerves will miraculously grow back or allowing yourself to become a chronic complainer or a dysfunctional and weak charity case. You can be bigger than your challenge by having and keeping a sense of humor, taking your rehabilitation seriously and doing the deep work that is necessary. Everyone has problems big or small. It just depends on how one chooses to deal with them. Your attitude choice is the core issue in determining a negative or positive, healthy outcome for your life. You are up to you.

Chapter 3

LOSS OF INNOCENCE:
Self-Preservation and the New Self

I find hope in the darkest of days, and focus in the brightest.
I do not judge the universe.
–Dali Lama

Coming to terms with your disability means losing your innocence. It is a right of passage and an initiation into a new and higher level of awareness and sensitivity. The moment-to-moment unfolding of events in the initiation process requires one to rely on one's self, measure the situation carefully, get information and safely guide the self through obstacles as they present themselves.

There is no ritual rights-of-passage in our culture. Initiation is more influential than a clearly defined event like a Jewish Bar Mitzvah. So as innocents we are left to ferret out and learn from those events that seem most meaningful and life changing. Our first love, first kiss, first heartbreak, a driver's license, graduation, first sexual experience, turning twenty one, getting fired, marriage, divorce, and so on, are all events that help us define our sense of maturation, belonging and being. In some tribal cultures there is a trajectory for coming of age. A boy is separated from his mother at a predetermined age, and brought into the company of men for the first time for a defined series of challenges, each designed and tempered to define the initiates new self awareness, self-concept and social stature. Coping with disability is another type of initiation.

OPERATING FROM YOUR ADULT, NOT YOUR CHILD

When we are thrown to the wolves of fate, we prevail or capitulate. If I was going to survive GBS, I needed to pay attention. This fact was demonstrated perfectly to me early on when in the local hospital. Two elderly "Candy Striper" volunteers accidentally dropped me on the hospital floor while attempting to transfer me to a gurney from my hospital bed. A part of me realized that I was not safe when the ladies were transferring me. All they were doing was changing the bedding, but they had decided to take me out of the bed, rather than the normal process of rolling the patient to one side, changing the sheet, then rolling the patient to the clean side and changing the other half of the bed. I should have said "no," but I didn't. I never reported the incident and although the staff knew about the incident, they said nothing to me. I still have back pain to remind me that I should have followed my initial instincts. I was initiated by default with that experience, one of many degrees of my initiation process.

Learning to trust myself and not to simply accept the process was important in my new situation. It was confusing, painful, scary and a real-time survival learning experience. My thoughts were, "This is not a dream, it is happening to me, it is dangerous and I need to step up for myself preservation. Could this be a gift in disguise?" Previously I had felt like a pinball, but now as experiences presented themselves, I chose not to simply allow myself to bounce off the challenge, but to pay attention and engage at a survival level. This was an initiation into a heightened way of being more present.

I recall lying on my hospital bed after the initial flurry surrounding the acute phase of my disease. My physicians choreographed everything for me during this initial phase. I felt my mind was relegated to the role of going along for a ride in my disconnected body. It was a feeling of disintegration, of being helpless in the face of so much "help."

At night I felt a kind of forced isolation. When my body was put to rest at the end of the day, thoughts of my new reality surfaced and occupied my mind. I had come to a crossroads in my life – a point when my existence as I knew it needed to die. With that death a new being would be formed through a purification process. I was being initiated into a new and higher consciousness. The shift from acute to chronic illness signaled a change from being cared for to self-care.

The most basic example I can share is when I discovered I was not drinking enough water, and I learned this the hard way by developing the most painful bout of constipation one can imagine. It was almost metaphoric as I was accepting everything and expressing nothing. I was not taking care of my most basic need, that of being aware of my body.

In the beginning, when I was lying completely paralyzed in my hospital bed in severe pain for days on end, I did not go to the bathroom for more than a week. The massive amounts of pain meds had paralyzed my gastrointestinal tract and I was now paying the price. In my suffering, I was in a drug-induced haze and had not been paying attention to myself and my natural needs. I knew that I had been eating more, but what I didn't know was that I wasn't drinking enough fluids. I was bound to have some type of major negative gastrointestinal episode; I had simply abdicated my biological needs to the care of the physicians and hospital staff. In the throws of really severe pain, I realized that the healing was to come from being aware of my own needs and acting to get them met by those who had charge of me. It was an epiphany caused by my lower GI track! It was going to be up to me to navigate through the labyrinth of my recovery process by sheer self-awareness and heightened conscious self-care. There was no neglect except what was caused by a lack of awareness on my part. It was at that point that I grew up totally; I realized that I held the tiller of my recovery and, for that matter, my life. That epiphany was life changing as it propelled me toward a full sense of responsibility for myself, even in my disabled state.

This meant that I was faced with giving up that pure, simple and naive part of me that functioned as an innocent kid. For me, this was not an easy thing to do. Part of being a good and creative artist is the ability to maintain a childlike take on life. The artist often takes the outsider's view, one of being out of the mainstream in order to view the goings on of life and report on them. Much like being a comedian who maintains a distanced perspective on life so that they can comment on it humorously, the artist comments artistically. It is also this childlike take on things, I believe, that allows us to abstract reality enough to be able to find humor, beauty, joy and uniqueness in the world, and report on it creatively in a way that is fresh and uniquely personal. In short, maintaining this childlike view is of real value. What doesn't work, and is quite different, is a childish view of things. This distinction is sometimes difficult to make. It is easy to blur the line between childlike perception and childish acceptance of the goings on around us. Everyone, regardless of whether you have an artistic temperament, shares this difficulty.

When my pink clouded perception of childishness was stripped away by trauma, the force of raw reality was life changing. It was a breakdown of everything I knew to be true; I was left unprotected and vulnerable to the tragedy playing out in my life. There are times in life when we find ourselves on paths that are not of our own choosing. There are philosophers that say we create everything in our lives and through our thoughts, emotions and desire – the laws of attraction – we bring disaster to ourselves. To me that belief flies in the face of logic. There are many things we draw to ourselves, but the jury is still out with regard to understanding cosmic chaos. It doesn't augur well in my mind to put all the responsibility on the victim. That seems to be a shortsighted blame-the-victim mentality. I have a hard time accepting it. What we can do is to take our mitigated assets after the trauma, collect ourselves and move heroically into the future.

IT'S A MIND-SET.

Feeling sorry for one's self is to be expected up to a point, but when there is no more new information and you are not using time for self discovery and healing, then it is no longer productive. It is then we can develop a mantra of "poor me" and get stuck. Being needless and "want-less" is a paralyzing state of mind. There is nothing that can really open up the possibility of progress like setting a goal, even a small goal. It is what moves us, energizes us and pulls us forward. An amazing amount can be accomplished when we have a goal. I believe the degree of happiness we experience is directly related to the quality of our goals. Usually the goals that we choose and which define our energetic motivation are ones that are not self-serving. However, my goal of healing was self-serving.

My initial goal set was to stay positive, chose to stay present and to realize I was very ill and not get lulled into complacency and acceptance of my circumstances. I wanted to learn as much as I could about my situation and put real energy and understanding into my recuperation. Goal setting was important; it helped me see my progress. I decided one of my simple goals was to outperform myself when it came time to do any kind of physical therapy. Also it was important to give myself credit.

This goal-oriented life choice is logarithmic, building on itself, gaining mass and expanding to others, serving to fill them with purpose and joy as well. Getting "unstuck" is hard work and starts with time spent in quiet, focused thought. There are plenty of welcome distractions to keep us off balance, offering us serial short-term fixes to our emptiness. For instance, entertainment empires are built on distracting us from healthy, introspective and nurturing thoughts. The real healing work begins when you tune into yourself and your needs.

The loss of innocence is an opportunity for a breakthrough in perception. It is like being held under a cold shower, gasping for breath, trying to adjust to the discomfort of a new unsettling reality. It may be brutal and there are many examples. When innocence is lost before the age of reason, it can cause permanent psychological damage. If lost after the age of reason, the loss and damage can be rationalized later in life and dealt with perhaps with some awareness, clarity and deep work. The wake up call comes as an abrupt change in a person's daily routine. In my case, I was living in a bubble and insulated from forced introspection. My innocence was based on a thought that I was immune from the kind of issues the challenged people had. I couldn't relate to being pulled out of the comfort zone of my life as I knew it.

We tend to fall naturally into ways of thinking, feeling, and being/doing. We all develop comfortable patterns within these three life elements. But essentially, we are really sleepwalking through life by following our unconscious thoughts. I recall while being at a very cool party in the Corralitos hills, full of artists, poets, writers, Zen practitioners, stoners, trekkers, sailors, and musicians (my crowd!), I had a conversation with a fellow who was a Buddhist. He said, "We go through life like we are taking a shower. We adjust the temperature of our thinking, feeling and doing. If we find ourselves thinking about something that is unpleasant, then we find a distraction to occupy our thoughts in that moment." This act is like adjusting the water in the shower so it's not too hot, or too cold. When we find our feelings are causing us pain or distress we find something to alter our state of feeling. Some turn to mind-altering substances, but the majority just gets lost in human doing rather than in human being. This can mean occupying ourselves with mindless activity – the art of staying unconscious by adjusting these three elements in order to be distracted from our inner stuff by outer stuff.

We seek a comfort zone in this pattern of coping with our day-to-day life whether we are happy or unhappy. Patterning is a natural thing to do. So, perhaps it is unnatural to be satisfied and complacent. Maybe the only way to truly grow is to be re-birthed and spanked into life through trauma.

The realization that I was caught up in a drama much larger than my-self – one in which I had absolutely no power or control - was a cold slap in my face. In my new life as a challenged person I was now a piece of flotsam in a stream, and I didn't know where I was going. I needed to wake up, heighten my awareness level and pay closer attention to everything. It was a profound breakthrough for me to ask questions and learn about my new life situation.

To me there is value in what I experienced. But it will only have real and practical worth if I can share what I learned with others. As I think about the initiation process, it seems that there is an element of expulsion, then isolation, followed by fear of the unknown and mystery. A dawning of self-reliance through self-discovery succeeds that. Assurance is gained by victory over doubt and thoughtless reaction. Ownership of success over the challenge will lead to celebration and a sense of knowing, with a new and powerful level of acceptance of self.

Much like any other type of problem solving, the answer will reside in clearly defining the problem. A healthy introspection can do this. An answer may be found in the way we tend to isolate ourselves when we are sad and hurt. It is during these existential periods that our skin is peeled off so we can discover what is real for us. Our wounding activates a deeper, transpersonal process of potential healing and illumination that we could not have initiated by ourselves. We have to go through the wound to re-ceive its blessing. But remember, there are some traumas that benefit from trained professionals so don't be afraid to ask for help.

Chapter 4

OLD PATTERNS:
The power of "NO"

It is not God's will merely that we should be happy,
but that we should make ourselves happy.
—Immanuel Kant

When I was in the acute phase of my disease, only family members could get access to see me. While in this time frame I received two and a half shopping bags of get-well cards from friends, coworkers and others from whom I didn't expect to hear.

As I stabilized, I was taken out of the Emergency Room and moved into the Intensive Care Unit. These environments are still very rarified atmospheres and hard for non-family members to penetrate. There was a period where I didn't see anyone other than immediate family. But once I was released from the local hospital and admitted into rehab, I had visitors whether or not I wanted them.

I was still in so much shock that I hadn't come to grips with what had happened to me. I was told what disease I had, but didn't really "get it" yet. By "get it" I mean the gravity of my struggle. I had many visitors initially and I suspect there was a lot of love as well as a healthy curiosity about my condition. At first I loved to see familiar faces, and be surprised by who had made the trip to San Francisco to visit me. These sessions were usually about an hour and a half long. Those sensitive to my condition would usually leave when they could see signs of my fatigue.

Before long, however, I began to actually dread visits, and I wasn't sure why. In retrospect, I think the sight of someone from my previous healthy context served to remind me of my dire situation, also their shocked expressions didn't help. Spiritually I was in a fearful and depleted state and welcomed a variety of religious groups who would visit hospitals and minister to people. These meetings also became tedious after a while. I felt they were doing this activity more for themselves than for me. I realized that I would feel quite drained after a visit. Still, I thought I should be strong for my loved ones. I put on a happy face and tried to make them think I was coping and healing. This was a false act that cost me dearly.

THE IMPORTANCE OF "NO" IN SELF-CARE

These acting sessions got old fast. All my energy was drained from socializing rather than being used for healing. I was conflicted. I wanted to see my family, but, at the same time, extensive visits with them would cause me to be exhausted for days. I spoke to my primary care nurse, Nancy Manos, RN, about these tiresome visits and she told me to simply say, "I am not up to it, I'm sorry." She told me to take care of myself and save my energy for healing. She gave me permission to be weak so that I could be strong again. It worked.

I needed to learn how to say "no" for my own welfare and to stop acting like I was OK. At that point I started to be more realistic about my time for visits. I visited with those who I knew, wanted to see, and only when I wanted to see them. It was empowering to be able to control, at last, my expenditure of energy.

SAYING "NO" TO FAMILY

As a kid I recall going to various friends' homes. To me it was interesting to see the difference in my friend's home environment. Some homes were clean and tidy, some were chaotic and noisy, some were sparse and others replete with material possessions. All my friends were fun, but the differences in their home environments bred different ways of perceiving the world from kid to kid. Some of my friends were optimistic, others were not. Their way of meeting the world was formed by looking through the lens of their home environment, and with each distinct view came a skill set for working through the unique, perceived challenges of their world.

As I matured and started to have more intimate relationships, I was amazed to discover that people not only chose others to reflect themselves so that they may grow, but that often their choices contained a component of familiar pain. The haze of our childhood and the context in which we grew up can often cloud our thinking as adults. People get comfortable in dysfunction; or perhaps they don't realize they can live without it.

Familial pain is an unconsciously learned way of perceiving the world. It's a condition much like the warm water that slowly gets hotter and hotter and finally boils the ever-adjusting, unconscious frog. Dysfunction is often not seen by any of the family members. It seems normal. It could be compared to growing up with a certain religion. We are brought up to believe and accept certain existing elements in our family as being normal, the way things are and the way they should be. As an example, if you have an expressive, shouting and argumentative family, you will think that this is normal. If you grew up in a reserved or polite context in which things could be rationally discussed quietly, then that would be your normal. "What's a good Christmas dinner if no one breaks a whisky bottle over someone's head?" This is, of course, a ludicrous example, but demonstrates that all human relationships are relative, and what we accept as normal may seem absolutely intolerable and outrageous to others. So, dysfunctional people may couple with other dysfunctional people because their behavior seems to fit so well with what they already know. It is "familiar." Also, if poverty and chaos seem comfortable, then that may be chosen. Crazy people find "normalcy" boring, and "normal" people find crazy people scary!

People get stuck in problematic relationships and stay in this constant familiar state of angst. Again, the angst is familiar so it sticks. It is only with heightened awareness, which may be brought forward by pain that we can be re-birthed into a new and peaceful life that contains the emotions that work for the new you. Our choices are tools by which we can form a pleasant reality. When we realize that, we can make the right choice, which will yield a level of empowerment. Life should be happy. The process goes something like this: In pain there is awakening of awareness. With awareness there is insight leading to knowledge. Knowledge is power, so one may take action toward a goal. With a mission of understanding and compassion for yourself and others, there will be peace.

FOLLOW YOUR INSTINCTS FOR SURVIVAL.

Veronica and Raymond were looking forward to taking her brother Gregorio to dinner for his 30th birthday. Gregorio wanted to go to San Jose to the De Anza Hotel where there was a fine Italian restaurant. Veronica didn't like the idea of driving from Salinas because it would mean driving back late at night. But when she mentioned it to Raymond, he said not to worry, he would be the designated driver which was the only way to go because Gregorio would be celebrating and drinking. Veronica reluctantly agreed and plans were made to pick her brother up and head to San Jose around 5:30 for a 6:45 reservation.

Veronica was in her sixth month of pregnancy and, as a result, she was uncomfortable sitting for long periods of time. She had already had two children: Raymond Jr. who was 10 and Angela who was eight. They had a happy life together, and all looked good for having a third child. Raymond had a job as a janitor at the local high school and was able to provide health insurance for his family. He was mechanically inclined so he did auto repair work on the side for extra money, which allowed Veronica to be a full-time mom.

On the night of Gregorio's birthday, the children were dressed up, and they all went to pick up Gregorio as planned. To their disappointment, Gregorio had been already drinking tequila and smoking marijuana. They didn't know how much of either he had had. They couldn't say anything in front of the children about the pot smoking, but Veronica and Raymond let Gregorio know they were disappointed that he had been drinking. The evening was supposed to be a family outing.

They arrived at the De Anza Hotel on time for the reservation and had a nice dinner except for the fact that Gregorio seemed to be high on something else in addition to the pot and tequila. He seemed to be unhappy that at thirty he was unmarried with no romantic prospects. When the dinner was finished, some of Gregorio's San Jose friends started showing up to see him and buy him more tequila shots for his birthday. By this time in the evening the family was ready to go home, but Gregorio wanted to stay with his buddies. The evening was ruined when Raymond tried to stop Gregorio's friends from getting him any drunker. He explained that he had his family and pregnant wife with them and he didn't want Gregorio to get crazy. Gregorio's friends "steam rolled" Raymond. Finally, Gregorio begrudgingly left his friends in the lounge in a drunken, drugged and angry mood.

The evening was pleasantly warm. It was relatively early for the adults, but late for kids. The children were in the back seat with Gregorio. Raymond and Veronica were in the front. About a half an hour into their drive home, the conversation degenerated into an argument between Raymond and Gregorio. According to Gregorio, Raymond was "pussy-whipped" and let his wife push him around. According to Raymond, Gregorio was selfish, childish and a loser. The argument peaked as they entered a stretch of undivided highway, and Gregorio started punching Raymond in the back of his head. He continued punching and then grabbed Raymond around his neck in a choke hold.

Raymond lost control of the car as it was going about sixty miles an hour. The car crossed over the center divider and crashed head-on into a passenger car instantly killing both people in the other car. The cars were a mangled tangle of metal, plastic and glass. Gregorio died of a head injury at the scene. The ambulance took surviving family members to the hospital where Veronica lost her baby. Raymond had cuts and a broken leg, arm and ribs. Raymond Jr. had a broken arm and some cuts and Angela escaped with minor injuries. This terrible accident also left Veronica with a broken back and confined to a wheelchair for the rest of her life.

I met Veronica in the rehab hospital, when she was in a body cast up to her chin. She cried a lot when I first met her. The loss of her baby, the death of her brother and the two others killed in the other car took a heavy toll on her. She always seemed to be looking upward with tears rolling down her cheeks; those are my final memories of her, a suffering Madonna. She realized too late that by accepting her brother's bad behavior, that she had jeopardized herself and her family. She was sad because in her heart and soul she knew that they should have canceled the evening. This brief lack of maternal strength and follow-through taught her the hard way to listen to her inner voice. We can be good parents and follow our instinctive compass in order to protect our loved ones and ourselves if we just listen to our inner voice.

HONOR AND BE CONSCIOUS OF OLD PATTERNS.

We have to be aware and beware of patterns that are invisible to us. Objectivity is impossible when our thinking is clouded with emotional residue. Clouding can result from a demanding parent pulling old strings, a variety of uncategorized feelings, or acquiescing to the needs of a selfish friend at an inappropriate time, i.e. like when you are in the hospital.

Let's look at "no" a bit more. We've all heard the funny quip, "What part of 'no' don't you understand?" My experience has taught me that saying "yes" is usually a lot easier than saying "no." A rhetorical "yes" that only gives you temporary relief in pleasing the other person is not a solution. Immediately we know we have betrayed our personal boundary just to make peace or "people please." What is left is a check we have written with our tongue that our spirit doesn't want the other party to cash. Of course, the check is instantly cashed and our self-esteem account balance takes a hit. We are left with a silent residue of remorse after having failed to honor ourselves by being honest about our real needs.

But how do we put "no" into practice? Sit with the request long enough to consider your needs and give an authentic answer. We add to our sense of balance and wholeness by not responding with a mindless "yes." In terms of a process, self-regard can be compared with the feelings of rising anger. If we can sit with the anger for a moment, we can discover where the anger originates, and understand why we get angry. We control anger by pausing for brief analysis, we may do the same with self-regard and saying "no." Make authentic conscious choices, feel good about it, then feel the mild tingle of the beginnings of real self-empowerment.

I recall asking a friend of mine for something. His answer was "absolutely not." I found this a powerful exercise in his defining his personal needs. His delivery took me back a bit, but I felt a sudden feeling of respect for him. He did not hesitate even for a moment to communicate his needs. He was very skilled at this concept of keeping his needs at the forefront of his consciousness. Perhaps as a good businessman he learned this survival skill so that negotiation would be minimal, or with this terse response the person he was dealing with would be forced to persist and prove to him their position and needs. Taking the time to analyze a request from a family member or friend and figuring out what you want, is healthier than offering a knee-jerk "yes."

LEARNING TO SAY "NO."

Our hope to protect ourselves from ill-timed demands from others lies in training ourselves to be more conscious. Upon hearing an inappropriate request, we must pause for a moment and hold onto self-care and self-respect. If you fail to heighten your awareness, you will be left abandoned with a wrecked journey of personal growth while the other party completes their "hit and run."

Practice it and in time you will feel better, and things in your life will start to fall in line. Introduce yourself to the lion in you. This is not easy work and to say that I have completely mastered it would be a lie. I do know I am more aware of this process, have practiced it, and it becomes easier to do. Appreciate the small steps you make and honor your achievement however small. You will discover a sense of self-empowerment every time you are able to hold back from capitulation for a moment longer than previously. Being aware of this process and using it as a tool is a worthy and incremental step toward grabbing the tiller of life and steering yourself in an authentic direction toward your personal needs and aspirations.

John Bradshaw, American educator, counselor, motivational speaker and author is credited with popularizing the idea of the "wounded inner child." This is a powerful conceptual metaphor for self-healing. To me this inner child is the part of us: the undeveloped and even damaged self-concept, which is formed in early childhood. The awareness of this idea allows us to become an advocate for that part of us which has been stunted. The use of "no" is the key to healthy boundaries leading to the creation of one's authentic self. Perhaps we weren't able to finish casting our sense of self fully when we were small. One could speculate that we were trained to put the needs of others before our own, possibly to an unhealthy degree. Finally learning how to say "No!" defines what our needs are, and ultimately helps us to define who we are.

BREAK THE MOLD AND CRACK OPEN A POWERFUL GRACE-FILLED YOU.

What can you realistically expect from yourself at this point? If you are like me, you probably were disoriented, helpless and passive at first. I was on a path that was directed for me. I didn't choose it, yet there I was on it. Realistic expectations of yourself will be revealed based on how you feel emotionally, physically and spiritually. Only you can measure this, and this measure takes knowledge of self. This knowledge of self will not only help you to survive, but also enable you to grow into a bigger person, a greater spirit, and a symbol to others of what a person is capable of doing in the face of personal annihilation. I expected that I would survive. The gifts I received from the life-altering challenge I faced surfaced later as by-products of my singular existential journey. A psychic wound can break the mold and crack open a new and powerful grace-filled you. This is not easy work. Just living with your new limited self is a challenge, but meeting and exceeding that challenge is what makes you a gift to other human beings.

Perhaps art therapist Peter London best sums of this process in his book *No More Secondhand Art.* He writes:

We are always in the process of becoming new, but because our minds are more facile at exercising memory than imagination, we fail to recognize this evolutionary quality in our life. Each morning upon rising we remember the person we were yesterday and form ourself in this new day more or less along the same lines of the way we were. We do this, even though the person we were is not always the person we prefer ourselves to be. Memory requires merely dogged constancy. Imagination, by contrast, takes courage and confidence in the rightness of our creations; hence its rarity.

Chapter 5

THE DARK ELEVATOR:
Courage, Patience and Self-reliance

Contact with my own species has always disappointed me,
solitude gives me a freedom of mind and an independence of action.
—Captain Nemo, Nautilus.

Maybe the following elevator story is a metaphor for self-care through patience, moderation, a bit of healthy resignation and faith in a positive outcome. What do we do when we find ourselves isolated from others and in the dark? It is then that we are challenged to draw from deep within our being a healthy calmness and contemplate our situation. If our first reaction is to panic we lose power to mentally diffuse the situational charge and switch into a mode of thought that allows us to plan strategies that can help us. Often we need to let go of the outcome and have simple faith that we will be OK. If we cannot control the situation then thrashing about in angst is a recipe for anger, spiritual destruction and maybe madness.

Things will start to fall into place after awhile. Your singular experiences will speak to you in new and clear ways. Whether you are recovering from a disability and/or trauma or not, I am referring to how we choose to react in any dangerous position or interpersonal situation. When things get unpleasant and challenge our emotional balance, it is crucial that we do not get sucked into the drama of others. I recall a situation when I spoke these words: "I'll never do that to myself again." What I meant was that I didn't want to repeat a mistake by losing control of my conscious awareness. I would suggest that anyone recovering from a traumatic experience should start keeping a journal. Look at the pages in your journal every once in a while. You'll see that as you read old entries, a pattern of behavior will emerge. In re-reading my own journal, I often found myself saying, "Oh, I was naïve and taken advantage of because of my preference of being liked at the expense of being respected." Your experiences, and those of others, will reveal universal truths to you. You will realize that certain things you already knew can be elevated to working tools in your life. I learned some important ways to care for myself. For example a simple tool is what I call "Shame on you, shame on you, shame on me," you may have heard this. This tells us to be aware of how many times a person disappoints you. The first offense is forgiven for now you know of the transgression and forgiveness is noble. The second offense "shame on you" you are let down to see that there is a pattern of disappointment and you are now made conscious of it yet forgive. The last "shame on me" is you taking responsibility for yourself and ending disappointing behavior from that person. You have allowed this person to repeatedly mistreat you and it now stops. Most of these strategies came to me by being buffeted around by individuals until I understood that I was worth taking care of.

Perhaps one learns to self-neglect as a child by being neglected or by being taught to believe that one's needs and feelings are not important. But one can practice and develop healthy boundaries, self-defense and realistic expectations with consistent practice. Similar to the process of learning to play a musical instrument, the notes, harmonies and tone of your life will improve with diligence and time. It might strike you suddenly that you have changed a pattern and are now empowered and validated in your effort to not only heal and restore yourself from your trauma, but to create balanced life experiences for yourself. When this happens, it's time to give yourself permission to do and say new things for your own well-being.

ABOUT COURAGE, PATIENCE AND SELF-RELIANCE.

I was in hospitals for seven months from the time I was stricken with Guillain-Barré Syndrome to the time I was released and fitted with a power wheelchair. The first few months I was a "high quad" which meant that all I could do was turn my head from side to side. I was fortunate that my paralysis was arrested by plasmapheresis treatments. At that time plasmapheresis was still an experimental treatment, but I agreed to "sign" a waiver so my doctors could do the procedure. I elected to use artificial plasma to be safe from AIDS. I never had a tracheotomy or was put on a ventilator to allow me to breathe. During this period my physical therapy consisted of passive range of motion exercises. This procedure was done so that my joints would not freeze up and my muscles would not contract. This went on for the first two months during the acute phase of my disease.

It took months of therapy before there was any measurable improvement in my range of movement. Being able to shrug my shoulders was the first return of anything I had lost and I was overjoyed.

When I graduated to and was fitted with an electric wheelchair it was like getting my first tricycle! Others had moved me about for months in an ambulance, various vans, Hoyer lift, gurney, or wheelchair. The prospect of independence of movement was exciting. My immobility had lasted much too long as far as I was concerned.

From flat on my back in a hospital bed, then to a tilt table in various degrees so my heart could get used to pumping blood, to my body in an erect position, then a standing frame, it was seven long months in rehab until I could be fitted to a power wheelchair. The occupational therapists fitted me with a set of slings so that my limp arms could be suspended from a spring over my right shoulder and a plastic piece on my right forearm and hand could be rested on a cuff that was attached to the control of the wheelchair. Once I got the hang of how to shift my weight a little, I could move the cuff forward, backward and side to side enough to move and direct the power chair. With a slight push forward of my right shoulder, my hand, which was suspended like a marionette, could click my wheelchair forward, backward, and around. The newfound freedom of mobility was exhilarating. I was able to visit patients in their rooms, go to therapy appointments and even go outside into the sunshine. This was a huge "step" forward.

One of the early educational experiences I had in my power wheelchair happened one evening when I used the elevator to look for a get together organized by the Occupational Therapy Department. I exited the elevator and my wheelchair clicked and hummed down the hallway anticipating a social evening with other patients. I entered the department and was surprised to see Téa, the beautiful Tahitian receptionist, was gone. The place was dim, quiet and vacant with empty therapy mats and rehab equipment stored away. Then I realized that the get-together was not in the O.T. area as I expected, but had been changed to the hospital cafeteria. As I turned to go the cafeteria upstairs, my eye caught site of a large window at the end of the main hallway with a view of a steep hill and quaint Victorian homes built side by side. I stopped to enjoy the sight of the old gals in various stages of repair and disrepair, some new with make-up, and some in desperate need of a face lift. It was dusk and lights starting to appear here and there. Sparse stars twinkled dimly in the cerulean blue evening sky. A solitary old gentleman slowly half-stepped his way up the steep sidewalk, resting from time to time by a pole or tree. It was a peaceful evening. The machinery of the hospital had slowly come to a grinding halt and the employee parking lot had emptied out – only a few arriving night visitors were securing their cars against the city night's unknown.

As I rounded the corner toward the elevator I decided, for some reason, to stop and take my left arm out of the sling by lifting and leaning my torso. I did this move without much difficulty; again I have no idea what prompted this thoughtless move. My arm dropped to my side on the outside of my wheelchair and came to rest with my hand next to the wheel. My muscle tone was still poor. It had not improved enough to lift my arm. To get my arm into my lap I started to swing my arm forward and backward like a pendulum. As I crunched my torso forward and back, my arm swung higher and higher until it was in front of me. At just the right moment it was my plan to turn my wheelchair quickly to the left, throwing my left arm onto my lap. With a click and a whirl I spun around and my arm landed with great success on my lap. Satisfied I clicked and hummed my way toward the elevator. I didn't notice that the support bar had shifted and was now facing behind me backwards like a tail. At the end of my tail was a two-inch foam square, which served to protect the caregiver's eyes.

I approached the elevator and hit the large up button and the door opened automatically. I lurched forward easily into the elevator and the doors quietly closed behind me. I maneuvered around inside of the elevator and punched the third floor button to join my friends. But when I hit the button nothing happened. I looked up at the elevator doors and noticed the square piece of foam from my arm support was tightly lodged between the two doors, out of my reach. This made the doors jam. The elevator would not work. I was stuck. Just then the lights in the elevator went out, leaving me in total blackness.

I realized that I was in trouble and would have to do something to help myself. I felt a chill of panic go up my spine. I had to dislodge the phone from its cradle somehow and hope it would signal someone that I was stuck in the elevator. I tried to reach the phone but I couldn't lift my mostly paralyzed arms high enough. I couldn't see anything but a faint glow from the Occupational Therapy floor through the small crack in the door of the elevator. Nevertheless, the dim glow was enough to help my eyes adjust to the dark. I leaned over toward the phone and, after several tries, I headbutted it off the hook. The phone jumped off the cradle and fell to the floor of the elevator with a bang. I could hear the dial tone but I could not reach the buttons. Then, the tone stopped. I had no other recourse but to holler as loud as I could that I was stuck in the elevator. That didn't work, either.

I looked for the emergency button and saw that it was out of my reach on the control panel. I pressed the third floor button again and again with my forehead but could not get the door open or the car to move up or down. After about twenty minutes of jockeying my chair around in the elevator I realized my efforts to gain help were futile. I could not work the phone; the buttons were out of reach, the phone receiver lay mute on the floor, and no one could hear me.

At that point I did what any person would do, I took inventory of myself; I wasn't thirsty, hungry or in need of the bathroom. I was warm enough, so I decided that perhaps the worst thing that could happen was that they would find me in the morning, asleep in my chair. I sat there for a few hours just relaxing and enjoying the mostly uninterrupted time of silence and meditation. I reasoned that at some point someone would complain that the elevator wasn't working and I would be rescued, stiff, hungry but happy to be freed.

The experience was not fun, but it was balanced by my newfound independence and limited mobility. I chuckled as I realized I would have an interesting story to tell my friends – the adventure of being marooned in the elevator! That situation served me well. It taught me not to panic, to weigh my options and wait patiently for help. I am not sure if anyone heard the calls, but in three and a half hours I heard the elevator door behind me open and a custodian came in and freed me.

ABOUT PAYING MORE ATTENTION AND SELF-CARE.

When I was nearing the end of my stay at the rehab hospital, a group of us who were in electric wheelchairs took a trip to the San

Francisco zoo. It was our first outing in a public place. We gathered in the morning, got on the lift up into the van and our wheelchairs were locked down. It was an odd experience riding so high in a vehicle, and all I could see was the street. Fleischacker Zoo was not crowded and we went directly to the merry-go-round area, which was down a rather steep hill. We set off caravan style, all the wheelchairs buzzing, clicking and humming along at a safe speed. When I got to the top of the hill and started down, the weight of my body slumped forward, causing my hand to press forward on the accelerator. This caused the chair to accelerate too fast down the hill, and because I was leaning forward with no core strength to straighten up, I could not slow the chair down. I was out of control zooming down the hill. I started yelling as loudly as I could for someone to come help and remove my hand from the control so the chair would stop. A young fellow, who I later learned was a Marine, ran up to help and stopped me before I smashed myself into the brick wall or tipped the chair over and hurt myself. The Marine was my hero!

Once we were at the bottom of the hill, we approached the carousel. I'm not sure what our occupational therapist was thinking, but we were all lined up to watch her ride. I think she just wanted to go on the ride and really didn't think it through. She had a large basket of picnic things she was carrying for later, so she came over to me and tossed it onto my lap and walked away. With that my hand hit the controls again and lurched me forward, but in a circle as my hand was forward and to the right. Off I went right into a full 50 gallon garbage can. It tipped over and my wheelchair bulldozed it in a circle spewing garbage in a nice even manner. Soda pop cans, drink cups, uneaten food, diapers, paper napkins, and more, decorated the area next to the merry-go-round ride. Even though we all thought it was really funny, it was yet another out-of-control experience and I didn't like it.

It is important to be brave and try things, but it is also important to be careful of able-bodied people who don't consider how their actions may affect us. There was no malice intended by the therapist, but her lack of thought caused me fear and stress in my first public outing since my illness. I was beyond embarrassment and had been for months, so that was not an issue. But I learned that I need to always be completely present and consider what the outcome might be when someone was either moving me, putting things on my lap while in my wheelchair, as well as the possible dangers of the terrain I was covering in my chair, among many other considerations.

Chapter 6

CHANGES IN FORTUNE:
A call to direct your life, Now

It was character that got us out of bed, commitment that moved us into action, and discipline that enabled us to follow through.
—Zig Ziglar

As a victim of our unique trauma, in whatever form it comes, perhaps we have some responsibility. Perhaps it would be in dealing with our chosen mind-set after the fact. Do I take any responsibility for what happened? Did I set myself up in some way? Do I accept what happened to me and live in my present reality, or, live a bitter life basing all my value as a human on a dead reality, a person who "used to be." When we accept ourselves then we can authentically accept others, keep love or find new love. When we choose to let things go forever, we make room for and find new ways to enjoy our gift of life. To accept the change we adjust our perception of ourselves, then we grow fully into the here and now and get present. In my case, I had to bury my love of guitar playing, beach volleyball, hiking and, my absolute favorite, dancing. This insight came to me through my own experiences, but also by witnessing the fate of other patients.

GETTING INTO DANGEROUS SITUATIONS AND NOT KNOWING IT.
When I had progressed enough that I could be transferred into a wheelchair and pushed around by nurses, I could finally enjoy some mobility, go outside to enjoy the view of the San Francisco Bay, see Alcatraz, the expansive Golden Gate Bridge and best of all, hear the noises of life, smell the

fresh air and feel the warm sunshine. With this mobility came an opportunity to meet patients who were isolated in their rooms. These patients were more critical or had been recently admitted.

There are some stories we hear that touch us deeply and usually it is of damage to someone's innocence. When accidents happen there is seemingly no rational or redeeming aspect in it. Perhaps the only redeeming part of tragedy is we can see the circumstances of the event and gain its obscure lesson that can help us. We need to be aware and on guard now more than ever before in our life. With self-acceptance we can see our value and cherish our self. This allows us to protect our self and survive potentially dangerous situations.

Mike was 14, short for his age with the perfect body of a gymnast or ballet dancer. He had seen wrestlers at his school, practicing after his baseball practice. He was curious about the sport of wrestling. His practice ended early and upon leaving the gym he passed through the area where the wrestlers were gathered.

Mike, being a good sport and competitive, paused to watch and was challenged to wrestle by a kid who was bigger than him. Mike put his gym bag down and was led to a mat, which was quickly surrounded by other wrestlers. The other student named Roland was a year older and one of the best wrestlers in the school. Mike knew nothing about the sport, not even the object of pinning one's opponent on his back for a count of three seconds.

It all happened so fast that Mike was taken by surprise. The more experienced schoolmate pinned him down within seconds of starting the match. For Roland this little match was an easy ego boost and a way to show off his skills. Embarrassed, Mike now clearly knew what the point of the match was and challenged Roland to a second one. Roland had three advantages: he was experienced, taller and weighed more. Roland had seen a wrestler on television lift an opponent over his head and do a maneuver called a "body slam." He tried it on Mike. Roland picked up Mike over and awkwardly threw him down on his head. All of Mike's dead weight plus the force of the throw instantly broke his neck at his fourth or fifth cervical vertebrae.

Mike couldn't move or breathe. He was at death's door. The gym teacher had seen the whole episode unfold as he watched his best wrestler try out the maneuver on this unaware, helpless novice. He could see by the way Mike landed and his position after the throw that a neck injury had just happened. The gym teacher immediately called the emergency help number. As soon as the call was placed he ran out to the mat and discovered that Mike's breathing was seriously compromised.

It was only a matter of 12 minutes before the paramedics arrived and performed a tracheotomy. By this time the gymnasium had been cleared of all people except the coach, the principal and teacher who was advising Mike's parents of the "accident" over the phone. Mike was taken to the local hospital and, after stabilizing he was transferred to the University of California Medical Hospital in San Francisco. He was operated on and given a procedure called a "fusion," essentially to secure the vertebrae together at the point of injury. They then fitted him into a Stryker frame, a frame that holds the patient and permits turning and rotating at various angles and planes while keeping the patient's body perfectly still.

When I met Mike at R.K. Davies, I had progressed far enough in my rehab to be in a wheelchair and be moved around. I was wheeled into his room where he lay flat on his back. He was fitted with eye mirrors that reflected his eyes horizontally so he could see around his room rather than just viewing the ceiling. The only movement he had was blinking his eyes and shifting his eyes around. He could not talk, not even in a whisper because he was on a ventilator to help him breathe. I will never forget the image of his eyes. They seemed to be literally disconnected from his being. For me, the image was a metaphor of the separation of mind-body. His mental capacity was not in any way diminished – he was very aware of everything going on around him. One's brain may make it through trauma with a determined mind, but one's body may or may not make it.

Roland went on to excel in sports. He was an expert water-skier and became an aquatics performer at a water park somewhere. He was the star of the show. I heard that he was even in a film. I am not sure what happened to him after that. I always wondered if he ever had any guilt about taking advantage of a person and indirectly ending a life. Mike never spoke to me but his eyes said it all. If the eyes are the windows to the soul, then what I witnessed was a completely detached and fractured being. His eyes held terror. The mind-body connection and the mind-body disconnection in Mike was presented to me instantly and literally. I felt the acute gravity of his helplessness and fear. Sitting by Mike's side, the words "There but for the grace of God go I" meant more to me than ever before. We know life is a gift, but it often takes nearly losing life to really "get it." I imagined myself in Mike's shoes and I admit that momentary experience made me appreciate my own lot in life. My mind then played back the near misses I had: diving into a shallow pool and striking my head, diving into unfamiliar waters at Lake Tahoe and feeling a submerged boulder graze my chest... It was simple Grace that I had dodged disability or death earlier in my life. I could clearly see in Mike's eyes that he wished he were in my shoes. He was not going to be able to accept his new reality. I heard that after being released from the rehab, Mike died of pneumonia at sixteen years old. What a gyp.

Here we are and there is no going back. It takes our personal commitment to prevail over this life-altering disability and trauma. These are not comfortable times so we soldier on. It is the quiet personal moments of counting our blessings that help us prevail. Also, the Serenity Prayer comes to my mind here.

God grant me the serenity
To accept the things I cannot change;
Courage to change the things I can;
And wisdom to know the difference.

—Reinhold Neibuhr (1892-1971)

IT'S NOT A GOOD IDEA TO TEMPT FATE.

Later on, some of the rehab patients learned about a new patient from the conversations of the nursing staff. In a real sense we became invisible to the nursing staff, so as they went about their responsibilities, we overheard their conversations about everything from staffing issues and who was romantically interested in whom. Also of interest was the subject of what patient had recently been admitted, the new patient's accompanying story and the kind of cards that fate had dealt him.

The latest buzz amongst nurses and assistants was a young man named Matt. He was a triple amputee who had been in an accident and lost his right leg and both of his arms. I paid attention and learned as much as I could about him as I was anticipating meeting him. I had already visited patients in the cancer ward, the burn ward and in my own ward. It was a diverse population, young and old, of suffering humanity in all stages of healing and dissipation. I had heard that Matt was hard to be with and talk to because he was powerfully negative. I told my primary nurse Nancy that I wanted to meet him anyway. She said she would check and see if it was OK and then set up a visit.

The meeting day came a few days later. It was early afternoon when I was wheeled into his sunny hospital room. Matt was tilted up slightly in his bed. As I was wheeled in front of him, I noticed the obvious form of his body missing his leg under the sheet and bed covers. The surgical procedures had taken their toll - he had almost no shoulders. Then I noticed a piece of surgical tubing coming from his mouth. With a piece of tubing and other parts from here and there, the nursing staff had fashioned a hookah device with lighted cigarette standing vertically in it. He was having a smoke. As he exhaled, gray plumes of smoke made slow organic swirling patterns in the warm, smoky, urine and bleach-tainted air. I found beauty in the lingering drifting smoke patterns but not in the smell.

Smoking was one of Matt's few pleasures. His other pleasure was to have his penis washed by the female nursing staff. It was the only time he had any contact, so he would get an erection. The nurses were obligated to give him bed baths, and I heard comments from the Filipino nurses that they had to go through this uncomfortable process with him, as it was a part of their duties. Matt slowly looked at me with deep, dead eyes. As he focused on me through the haze of the pain medications, his eyes started to gain life again and in a few seconds there was a stoned look of curiosity on his face. We were introduced and had some small talk. But it took several meetings before he opened up and told me what had happened to him.

It was a sunny winter day in San Francisco. Union Square was crowded with people Christmas shopping. Macy's was in full decorative glory and the city's pace was brisk. The Holiday shopping season had started so sidewalks around Union Square were full. Matt was standing mid-block waiting for the bus, not really knowing or caring where the bus route was. He waited nervously, and, finally, several blocks away, he spotted one.

Matt had planned a life of comfort but he had not had any success no matter how hard he tried. He had decided that if he could collect a large sum of money from the municipal transportation system, from a lawsuit, he wouldn't have to work at all. If he were to make physical contact with a moving bus he could fake a serious injury. He thought that in actuality he would only sustain minor wounds and the lawsuit money would be well worth the inconvenience of some time spent in physical therapy. But perhaps, on an unconscious level, this was really his suicide mission. As the bus loudly lumbered up the hill he did not notice that it was out of service. He also didn't notice that the light at the intersection was now green. He calculated that if he stepped in front of the bus just as it pulled into the bus stop at a reduced speed, he could pretend he was injured and win his prize. Sadly, Matt stepped in front of the bus at the same time it accelerated to get through the intersection before the light changed to red. In an instant he was run over by the right front wheel and found himself under the bus, tangled in the wheel well. The bus continued through the intersection with Matt trapped underneath. The bus finally stopped after the driver heard Matt's screams – it had traveled half a city block. In just a few moments Matt had been transformed into a mangled mess of humanity. After many hours of surgery at University of California San Francisco Hospital, Matt woke up a triple amputee.

The story of his attempt to fake an accident and collect easy money circulated through the hospital staff and among the patients. As it turned out, he did not win the lawsuit and ended up with less than nothing. Here is a good example of how one cannot know what to expect when testing the unknown. In his head his vision was to have a minor injury, a lawsuit and a large cash settlement that would secure his retirement. What Matt got was the worst possible outcome of a failed plan. Also, his mind had been deeply scarred by the trauma so that he had become a spiritual "black hole." No one wanted to be around him in his state of mind. He was dark and toxic.

I tried to imagine myself in his body and in his situation. It wasn't that hard to do because I couldn't move my arms or legs, so in some ways we were similar. However, he had no hope of getting his missing limbs back, whereas I had hope that mobility would eventually return. It's true that he had it worse than me. Our two different points of view met each other, and I could see that his was shrouded in hopeless negativity.

Somewhere out there in this world is a man with only one leg and no arms trying to figure out what to do. If he even wanted to commit suicide he couldn't do it without assistance. I learned from Matt that the universe is already in balance and it is not wise to try to manipulate the unknown. It always hurt and amazed me when I observed what Matt had done to himself. His situation was very different from when life randomly presents us with a challenge. I can only imagine what traumatic thoughts he had about what he had done.

Chapter 7

FINDING LOVE:

Those Who Hurt You Can Also Help You

That which does not kill us serves only to make us stronger.
—Friedrich Nietzsche

Is it possible that this dramatic change that has happened may have some element of opportunity? I learned it's how one chooses to look at it. In American society surface appearance is king. From automobile design to food packaging, everything is a product to be marketed. The surface image of the product is what this culture seems to judge value by. Our physical bodies carry our spirits, but, unfortunately, our spirit cannot be seen directly, although our facial expressions and our eyes are huge clues. In my wheelchair I noticed that people would avoid eye contact with me as though they might be adversely affected by connecting with me. I became invisible to many people and I found this painful. I also learned that many people thought that because I was in a wheelchair that I must be mentally deficient. Rather than getting angry, I had compassion for them. They pre-judged me as defective based upon my particular packaging. Disabled or not, I was the same soul, just awakened in a new way after my trauma.

While I was living in Soquel, California, I had a very nice home with many extras like a wine cellar, a hidden safe and more. The builder built it for himself, when things got financially tight for him he had to sell it. We added an elevator and remodeled the bathroom to be ADA compliant for me. It had a beautiful roll-in shower room with small pale terra-cotta fish scale tiles and large floor to ceiling plate glass mirrors and windows. Ultimately we lost the home due to lack of income. I couldn't work for two reasons: I was disabled and I was receiving Social Security Disability payments.

From my home I used to drive my power wheelchair about four miles to the Capitola Beach. My chair battery was good for about ten miles plus. I would enjoy the ride from Soquel to Capitola and arrive to sit on the esplanade breakwater and look at the sea and watch the activity on the beach, particularly volleyball and Frisbee. I was a disabled person who had experienced near death and all kinds of suffering and still had the desire to be around physically unchallenged people on the beach. I noticed that as I was cruising along to find a nice spot with a good view, only children would look me in the eyes. Kids seemed unencumbered by boundaries. They would look at me, smile at me and even engage me in conversation.

Parents and others would look away like insecure people who don't make eye contact and need to prep before engaging. I thought the "look away" might be based on some guilt they had for being healthy. Or perhaps it was a visceral response that I might be contagious if acknowledged! After observing this behavior numerous times I gained some objectivity and came to a conclusion: I realized, without anger or judgment, that I had so much to offer as a human being because of the profundity of what I had been through, that others were selling themselves short by dismissing me.

THE IMPORTANCE OF CONNECTION, LOVE AND SUPPORT.

Huck lost both his parents and a brother in an automobile accident when he was 9. At that time his life was already rough enough. He had been diagnosed with infantile paralysis that affected one arm and a leg. As a polio victim he had been hospitalized numerous times and the medical community did all they could to correct the polio and help him become pain free. Because of his short leg, his back was off center and he suffered from sciatica and lower back pain. When Huck was 12 he had his first back surgery. This was the beginning of so many operations that he told me he had lost count of them. He had also lost three inches in height over the years. Huck's destiny was to become a human guinea pig. Since he had no parents, those who were indifferent to his emotional welfare made the decisions for his medical care. If there was an individual who needed to try a new procedure, Huck was an easy choice.

In his youth Huck became a ward of the state somewhere in the Midwest. He only had a second cousin who he could call family. Poverty and being an orphan kept him from having the loving environment that a family can provide. His cousin had a daughter who would contact Huck from time to time when she had no one else to go to and was in need. He spoke very fondly of her; she was his family.

Huck developed a warrior's countenance and learned and accepted that his life was going to be a hard one. He endured challenges, essentially had no emotional support and those who befriended him were short-term captives of the hospital and rehabilitation system. His personality was a strong one and he was fair-minded. He was a character of few illusions. At an early age he learned he was on his own and his only true advocate. Huck was a realist and fatalist, yet hopeful at all times. Hope was his sword; trust his shield. Despite his years of suffering, he was still nourished by the prospect of one day being pain free. To me he was an invincible spirit and a role model. Huck never complained, but he had a way of being very clear about what his needs were.

I knew him because he was my rehab hospital roommate for a while. When I met him I think he was about 65. I recall he was prescribed the intravenous blood thinner Coumadin. No one is sure how it happened, but the electrical plug on the dispensing unit had dislodged from the wall socket. This led to the unit dispensing a free flow of medication into his body all night long. In the morning when the staff discovered what had happened, he was near death. But before long his vital signs returned to normal – a testament to his incredible strength. He had many near-death experiences; most people rarely experience one.

Huck's approach to surviving in a hospital was to assume that everyone was completely incompetent. Two types of people populated staffing: healers who were gifted, and those who were there to get a paycheck. He had learned at an early age to judge those who would help him or hurt him; he also learned to take care of himself in what he decided was a hostile environment.

At one point Huck's niece called him and promised to come visit him. He spent the next couple of days in excited anticipation. It would be the first time in years that he would see her. The appointed weekend came and went without any word from her. After visiting hours on the evening she was supposed to visit, Huck withdrew to his hospital room. That evening he did not eat dinner. He did not want to speak to anyone.

Around three in the morning I heard the intercom and pager announcing a "code blue." When the only person he cared for, and the only family he had, did not visit him as promised, Huck had enough. They discovered Huck's body in the bathroom. He had fallen and struck his head fatally on the rim of the toilet bowl. I heard footsteps running in the hall and staff speaking in urgent but hushed voices. The doors of all the patients' rooms were systematically closed with no explanation. He said goodbye to no one. There was little said about Huck after his death. The story of his life is a sad one, full of suffering and disappointment. He held up to immense challenges throughout his life but he did not die from his physical ailments, but from a broken heart.

Though it's good to be independent, we can all use someone to care for us. Still, the lesson here is that we must be conscious of how and why we attach ourselves to others. The path to love can be a bumpy one regardless of your disability, so it is of the utmost importance to maintain a guarded awareness of yourself and others in your search for understanding, acceptance and affection.

USED TO BEING LOVED, ADORED AND ATTACHING UNCONSCIOUSLY.
There were various teachers and helpers on my journey: doctors, nurses, therapists, family, friends, hospital patients and love interests good and bad. I started learning during the acute phase of my injury and continued to learn into the chronic phases and well beyond. While I was in the hospital, my antennae were up. For survival I learned about how I was cared for and how I could care for myself. After I was released from the rehab hospital the lessons changed as I experienced a new way that people perceived me. It is interesting to look back now and acknowledge the individuals who helped me grow. People had a lesson to teach me and each helped me in a way that often was not known by them or by me at the time. Pain, rejection, isolation and disintegration are all teachers and often the deeper the wound is, the more one can learn. It is hard to see another human being in pain whether it is by fate or their own ignorant doing. In a way, I learned to love my comrades in suffering. As individuals merged in and out of my life, I began to think of us as a unique family. Stripped of all the superficiality, we had no option other than to be completely authentic with one another and share our hopes and fears. When someone suddenly disappeared, we always wanted to know what happened to him or her. When a person ended up in the hospital due to bad judgment, it was possible to gain insight into my own situation by learning how fateful surprise or human folly can lead to tragedy. Early in my disability, there was a secret component of dread in my mind that perhaps I brought my situation upon myself from previous poor choices. Of course, that wasn't true. I had a

healthy list of unhealthy behaviors, which I eventually learned to correct as I re-entered life outside of the rehab hospital.

My marriage to Susie started to falter. The issues I had with my self-esteem began to manifest in obsessive-compulsive behaviors. My insecurities about my self-image created behaviors that served to push her away from me. In retrospect even though I had learned so many lessons, I still had not made the step to have these lessons play out in constructive ways and my actions served to position her so I would be abandoned. Like a self fulfilling prophesy my insane way of dealing with my personal issues served to accelerate the inevitable collapse of trust and love. At one point she said "I hate the one I love" and "I don't want to be married to you anymore." I had caused her so much pain that I pushed her out of my life. Perhaps at some level I believed I was doing her a favor so she would not be stuck with what I believed was a defective person. I made too many mistakes and was unredeemable. My alcohol abuse didn't help either. The marriage lasted 10 years before I killed it and we divorced.

Probably the most painful lesson for me later on was centered around a possible love relationship. I wanted to know if I was still "love worthy" in my disabled condition. I found that the lesson was about valuing my dignity and self-respect over being liked and accepted. I was emotionally beaten up by love interests: it seemed that their acceptance had various stages, but when it eventually came down to commitment, they could not get past my disability. There were many words of rejection, for an example when I was sick with the flu, "I didn't sign up to be your nurse." These painful words burned a brand on my heart that said I was defective and unworthy of love. Of course, I suffered deeply until somehow I had the insight that the shortcoming was not in me but in the insecurity of the love interest. They felt diminished because I didn't look normal or show well.

This life lesson ultimately has to do with judgment, expectations and self-respect. As I was being judged on my appearance, not my inner being, my love interests feared that they might end up being caregivers. There is a kind of selfish arrogance that comes along with this type of shallow judgment. The person making the judgment never considers that at any time they might be diagnosed with cancer, get injured and become the "other" like I am now.

This type of person is often looking for a target to express and work out their free-floating anger and frustration. Never underestimate the stupidity of some people. This behavior can come coated in warm and seemingly compassionate behavior. Once this type of person gets your confidence through favorable actions and words, it is just a matter of time until they hit a wall in their relationship with you.

Of course not all people are going to act this way, this is just an example of a type of person to look out for if you want to protect yourself. Be aware that, without your even expecting it, this type of personality may express all their unmet expectations and anger on you as a convenient target. These are the type of people who can't own up to their own dysfunction; they cannot see it; it would never occur to them. They see themselves as superior to you.

I learned from my disability to witness behavioral patterns in others. I learned this behavior was called the witness consciousness. To me witness consciousness means the ability to multi-task mentally. I mean function on two levels at once like being in it but not of it. As an example, say I am in a situation where the interaction with another is beginning to take on the character of a confrontation, or another is treating me in an offhand way. This way of thinking is described as being present in the conversation and interaction but at the same time able to look at it from a part of my brain that is detached, non-judgmental and unemotional. In short this view is just observing the interaction and looking for information that may help me understand the person without being drawn into it emotionally or from any ego oriented point that may serve to intensify the dynamics of the interaction. This allowed me to see the story play out and not be affected by, or be drawn emotionally into, the drama. You too can avoid being drawn into unpleasantness. In my personal relationships I have developed this practice. It is a type of detachment that cannot be recognized by another. It gives me an edge because I can stay in balance. This will help you by not getting drawn into a downward spiral of inter-action caused by a limited and reactionary point of view. In short it is a more sophisticated way of relating to others and particularly helpful when relations are strained and you are being "baited" by another. It is a valuable tool giving you an edge by being unemotional and not succumbing to knee jerk responses. It also has a calming affect on the other. Once this tool was developed, these people were seen as my allies who could help me through inadequacies and dysfunction. In many ways I benefited from both posi-tive and negative social and personal relationships. I found that I needed to be on guard and conscious while my heart searched for understanding, acceptance and love.

Manfred, a world-traveling psychic, met me in San Francisco. He was on the final leg of a tour reading people and giving them insights about their lives. He had a global route that he made several times a year. He would be returning to Bavaria after being in Italy, France, Australia, Japan, and other points unknown to me. The appointments were held in a furnished flat where he would see those who knew of his extraordinary talents. As usual I was a skeptic – the jury was out on him. My friend, Ed Teitcher, who was also an artist had an appointment ahead of me, so I waited for about 45 minutes in the living room while Manfred did my friend's reading. When my friend came out, I could see a change in his countenance. He seemed happy and at peace, whereas before the meeting he was very nervous and had chattered continually during the drive up the coast from Santa Cruz.

I had plenty of time to obsess about what was on my mind and was hoping that the session might shed some clarity on what was happening in my life. The door finally opened and a nice fellow of about 34 asked me into the dining room and closed the door behind me. I introduced myself and he did the same. He had a Belgian accent and seemed calm and poised. He had a casual elegance about him. I liked him right away. We sat across from each other at the dining room table, and he took out a deck of playing cards. He shuffled the cards a few times, had me cut the deck and then took a card from the top of the stack. At that point he looked into my eyes deeply and said, "Tell me of the queen of sadness." I was surprised he could so quickly read what was on my mind. His comment was about my first attempt at a love relationship after my disability.

After ten years of physical therapy, focused effort, and the very slow regrowth of my motor nerves, I was able to go from a power wheelchair, to parallel bars, to two Lofstrand crutches, a single crutch and then a cane. I was gaining strength and independence. I wore plastic ankle foot orthotics on both feet to help with "foot drop" as I was, and am now, still paralyzed from the knees down.

As my first outgoing venture I enrolled in a painting class called "The Outdoor Painter's Project" at University of California Santa Cruz. I was trying to re-enter the mainstream as best I could. In the painting class we would have numerous slide lectures and go out on location to paint outdoors rather than in a studio. During class, a lady caught my eye. She seemed to want to buddy up with me to paint, and ultimately, we became involved.

It was important to me to be lovable again, to prove to myself that I was attractive to the opposite sex, and able to function socially in an intimate setting. In my eagerness to be in a relationship, I accepted behavior that I never would have accepted before, just because my goal was to prove I could be lovable. I had promised myself that I would not tell this person "no." I became addicted to this person slowly without realizing it. But soon, I found myself in heart-wrenching pain rather than bathing in the warm glow of love and affection. I was focused on the needs of another, bowing to an unwritten agenda, and ultimately learned that she was sleeping with another man at the same time she was sleeping with me. That period of non-clarity would yield a life lesson – a painful, but important one. This woman hurt me emotionally, but in a way, she also helped me to understand that I shouldn't pretend to be anyone other than who I am in order to appear desirable to another.

After I talked to Manfred about my experiences with her, my hurt feelings, and disappointment, he continued in his collected way to outline what my situation was and why I had found myself feeling the way I did. As he spoke I could see the compassion in his eyes and feel his desire to help me. Before my disability, I would never have considered going to a psychic, and I am not necessarily recommending that you see one. I was open to all the knowledge I could receive. I am just saying that this person seemed to have a real understanding of me and he helped me make profound progress with a serious block when it came to engaging in a relationship.

Needless to say, I was shocked that Manfred could read me so fast. I had invested myself totally in making a love relationship work regardless of whether or not the person I was in a relationship with was even worth it. I was unaware that what I was really doing was trying to prove to myself that I could have a successful romantic relationship after having been through so many traumas. I was in love with the idea of being in love and in a relationship; it had little to do with the woman. In fact, I had unknowingly done a perfect job of picking the wrong person, plus she had problems.

His comments were many and are lost to the indefinable collective wisdom in me now. The only specific one left with me is a lesson about self-respect and boundaries. He placed his hand on mine and said, "The first act of self love is to not let anyone into your life that doesn't make you feel good about who you are." It landed, it was perfection. I realized that I allowed this sadness in my life because I was making excuses for the person who I cared for– for her dysfunction and condescending behavior. My desire to be "love worthy" clouded my thinking. I tried to make that particular relationship work at the expense of my happiness. My lesson: I lost sight that love is happiness, not the quest for happiness at all costs.

This duty of self-love must be committed to and honored. This is the foundation for happiness and your peace of mind. Now, I see that Manfred's powerful words are applicable to any situation where we find ourselves torn apart at our deepest level. This may apply to a careless and troubled love interest, a family member, a friend, a nurse or a room partner in a hospital. Get them the heck away from you if they are toxic. Do it for your own self-preservation. Be moved to do this.

Manfred was an ally, and so was that love interest. The two of them helped me clarify a lesson that I needed to learn, and I did learn it. Ultimately, my failure to make self-valuing choices caused me a lot of pain. It wasn't that I didn't like myself per se, but I had been unconscious of the possible results of my self-diminishing choices.

I always loved the Groucho Marx quote: "I refuse to join any club that would have me as a member." That seemed to really sum up the degree of my self-deprecation in my love relationships. There was protection in choosing unavailable people. I could be guaranteed of being the ultimate victim, the "dumpee," and this fit into my previous unconscious behavior patterns.

I was finally and painfully learning that if a person with whom I was romantically interested exhibited any unpleasant behaviors then, I should move on, protect the little kid in me, and feel empowered by it. It was all a matter of awareness, and it was a by-product of sharpening my skills in reading others and myself. I got sick of saying "I'll never do that to myself again!" Being alone and thinking about these choices and behavioral patterns caused me to learn that I didn't want to repeat them. Being disabled was empowering me to take better care of my needs and feelings - it is what I needed to happen to attain a higher degree of personal growth. This was a powerful realization.

More than once, I experienced the hope of partnering and was thwarted by an invisible barrier to a romantic connection. We often tend to idealize our love interests, and in doing so, we can sell ourselves short. I rarely gave myself credit for the forced "prison term" of hours of introspection, painful growth and the resultant liberating enlightenment I earned while I was learning to function again. By keeping your emotional balance when in a positive or negative relationship, you can be like a trader on the stock exchange. Whether the market goes up or down, you can always profit by learning to view each positive or negative experience as an opportunity.

WHAT YOU SEE IS WHAT YOU GET. I CONNED MYSELF.

After that experience with the "Queen of Sadness" I became attracted to another woman. She seemed to really like me and appreciate my talent, personality and intellect. I graced her with time, gifts, poetry, and advice for relationships with other men, support after break-ups, and a lot of emotional support in tandem with unanswered affection. My hope was that the friendship would develop into a love relationship. She was sweet to me, appreciated me, and looked caringly into my eyes – but had no interest romantically. I was hurt when I couldn't get even the slightest warm reaction from her. We talked about it and she said coolly, "It could never be," but I was unable to hear, understand, and believe she just wanted me as a good friend.

I continued in my quest and at one point we became closer. I remember I was so happy because I thought we had finally connected. Later she said that she was just emotionally vulnerable then and that she was uncomfortable with the closeness. So in essence my highest point was her lowest, how humiliating. It was hard for me to accept because I am a really wonderful person!

It was easy for me to blame my disability for this ongoing lack of acceptance. So I persisted and unknowingly targeted this unavailable person to work my issues of apparent childhood neglect. I projected onto her and recreated how it was in relationship with my mother, never knowing where I stood one moment to the next and always trying to seek reassurance that I was loved.

I share this experience with you because it was a complex situation where I had more going on with me than just my disability. In short she was Ok with my disability, but not me as a love interest.

When we experience trauma as a pre-verbal child there are literally no words to describe feelings. These indescribable emotions remain in the unconscious mind waiting to hopefully land in a place of clarity later in life. My parent did the best she could to nurture me with the tools she had. I do have a treasured memory of my mother and I sitting in a lawn swing, in the sun, rocking me in her lap and caressing my head.

So on we go and it is blessed luck if we find somebody. Life may present us with a "perfect" partner who may become disabled, abandon us, or die an untimely death. How many spouses still love their loved ones after a trauma? Many. And the simple and elegant reason is that they know and love the person within. As couples get old together and face the "disabilities" of old age, they can still experience deep love because they know the person inside the body. How lovely.

FALSE STEPS ON THE PATH TO LOVE.

Trying to find a love interest may be really difficult for a person who has experienced a serious trauma or has a life-diminishing disease like multiple sclerosis. I have a disabled female friend who I have grown to care for over the years. She is sweet, intelligent, funny, edgy and attractive , but in my opinion she is also a bit spoiled, in reasonable denial, and angry. I have seen this friend be disappointed time after hopeful time by suitors who can't go deep enough to see that the disease is not the person. In her case, the romance always starts off hopefully, has a duration of several months, may lead to intimacy, then once the settling in period develops there seems to be a post initial romantic realization by her love interest that he has attached to a person with significant future limitations and needs. My point on this matter is that, even though we are all capable, it takes a very special person who can go deeper in a relationship to grasp and love the true essence of a person.

You will inevitably find yourself engaged in interactions that are unpleasant. That's life. You can help yourself find peace by maintaining your balance. This is achieved by using witness consciousness. Engage this mind-set by not being reactionary. Don't respond on a surface level. Sit with the situation. Put your emotions on the back burner and turn down the heat of the moment. Slow everything down and ask yourself a few questions. What am I feeling? How am I being treated? Is this worth it to me? Do I really need this? What are my options? In short it is easy to be treated off hand by others but deadly to your spirit to let yourself allow it. Be balanced, be dignified, be your new self it. Is your choice.

I found that I needed to be on guard and conscious while my heart searched for understanding, acceptance and love. Once you develop observational tools that allow you to step back from the situation, you will be able to find the right person for you. Quite by accident I found a person who is caring, thoughtful, and generous. I love her. She has enough life experience to know that what you can't see is actually what you get - a person's value goes much deeper than surface appearance.

GRIEVING THE LOSS OF THE FORMER SELF.

Personal rejection and dismissal is really painful. Usually this is because people put on a false face and don't have the depth of character, compassion or understanding to go deeper than the surface of a person. That is my opinion and is how I dissected my lack of acceptance by many. This feeling is shared by many and goes deeper than love relationships. Certainly people of different ethnic backgrounds and sexual preference feel lack of acceptance on a regular basis.

If you take rejection as a personal character flaw you will form a negative attitude. The self-concept that you are flawed in character rather than in physicality will keep you from transitioning through the healing stages of grief into the sunlight of self-love and power.

DENIAL

After disability or trauma one is unable to admit that the change is permanent. They may continue to imagine themselves as before. Instead they may deny their feelings and not admit their new reality.

ANGER

After disability or trauma, one feels angry about the pain of an inexplicable loss.

BARGAINING

After the anger stage, one may plead with a higher power, promising anything in order to reverse the damage or trauma. Example: "Please give me a chance, give me a miracle."

Depression

Next, one might feel discouraged that his or her bargaining plea did not work. This may spiral into depression, causing disruption to life functions such as sleeping, eating and self-care.

Acceptance

Moving on after disability or trauma is the last stage. One accepts that the old self is left behind and begins to move forward with his or her life. He or she may not be completely over the situation but is weary of going back and forth, so much so that they accept their new being as reality.

So, think beyond yesterday, appreciate it, learn from it and move forward. Like an Italian race car driver, throw away your review mirror. Learn about the five stages of coming to terms with the death of your whole physical body, the trauma of loss and do your grief work. It is not easy to do, denial usually being the key obstacle to any kind of breakthrough.

Chapter 8

HEIGHTENED HUMANITY:
Avoid Prejudgment

Moral excellence comes about as a result of habit. We become just by doing just acts, temperate by doing temperate acts, brave by doing brave acts.
–Aristotle

In the hospital I was guilty of the very kind of prejudicial behavior I would experience when I was released from rehab into the world. Living in a constant state of adaptation I spent long hours learning how to dress, feed myself and work with my limited mobility. All the self-determination and focus it took so I could accomplish the activities of daily living created in me a kind of keen self-absorption. I associated with people in a shorthand of surface perception and involvement. Perhaps it was a natural way of relating under the circumstances with shades of carryover from the way I related to people before my trauma. I learned this about myself as I found others relating to me in this way. How ya doin? Fine.

WHO AM I NOW AND WHERE AM I GOING?
It took me a while to accept that my role was now going to have me cast as the disfigured person who walks with crutches. I must admit that when I see myself at a bank in the video surveillance monitor, I am at first surprised by my image. I forget what I look like even though decades have passed since I became disabled. I still look at myself in the bathroom mirror and note my disabled body with amazement. My hands used to play the guitar, a Fender Stratocaster pre-CBS model, and now I can't because I

have no strength in them. I don't create music, but still enjoy music. I play a game in my mind knowing where my fingers go on the frets and how to play chords. I still have a song in my heart. It is a loss, but I am not lost.

I spent many hours on the Internet reading articles about trauma and adaptation. Also learning from YouTube videos. Many were very generous with information and I learned as much as I could about coping skills that might help me adjust to my new lot in life. I found the information presented by John Bradshaw, a U.S. educator, pop-psychologist and self-help movement leader a good fit for what I needed to learn and put into practice. I learned that what he called the "inner child" is our childlike aspect. It includes all that we learned and experienced as children, before puberty. The inner child denotes a semi-independent entity subordinate to the waking conscious mind.

The concept of the "inner child" has manifold therapeutic applications in counseling and holistic health settings. Bradshaw famously used "inner child" to point to damaging childhood experiences and the lingering dysfunctional effects of childhood coping skills that don't work in adult situations.

John Bradshaw goes further to introduce the nuance of the "wounded inner child" and encourages the adult to protect the inner wounded child, to become an advocate, and provide the kind of nurturing and balance that was not available in childhood.

The idea of being a kid inside and an adult outside helped me. I became aware that my choices were those of an adult looking out for the kid in me. It didn't happen all at once either, but once I was aware of this dynamic of complete self-responsibility, I could get the hang of it and make it work. Sometimes I found the expectations and mindless disregard that others had for me astounding. I often find myself laughing in appreciation of my newly acquired skills; skills that create self-protecting choices that lead to wholesome, fruitful and self-affirming behavior.

For example, I coproduced a program on the local community access television channel. The subject was about literary, culinary and visual arts in Santa Cruz County. I also interviewed musicians and had them perform live in the studio.

I was interviewing an artist at his home studio, which was located in his back yard and up a steep incline. I arrived with my video camera, tripod, lighting equipment and reflectors. I was amazed that the artist needed to be asked to help me unload and carry equipment into his studio. Even as a disabled person I was doing my part in the community to support and promote the arts. But he didn't have the awareness, experience or insight that he could help me help him. This was empowering to me. I spoke up and said, "If you would like to be interviewed, you will have to give me a hand with this equipment."

Don't indulge in shame.

Just because you may only have half a body left does not mean that you are not a whole person. In many cases a traumatic injury brings us to the full potential of our humanity. One of the first things we learn as a disabled person is that disability is not a communicable disease. We learn this by experiencing people who do not acknowledge us in public, avoid eye contact or overreact by over-helping us to the point of our discomfort and embarrassment. Disabled people have a name for this: we call it "help rape." I recall years in my wheelchair observing the behaviors of able-bodied people. It seemed that many people were asleep to their being and had a lack of awareness of the blessings of their intact physiology. In particular, I found it very disturbing to see morbidly obese people gobbling fatty foods. In my condition, with the lack of options I had, it was saddening to see someone with all their limbs and their nervous system fully functioning allow themselves to voluntarily degenerate into a state of ill health.

PREJUDGING INDIVIDUALS.

It's hard to get to a point of personal growth where we can get past our personal protection. The tendency to prejudge people is probably innate. We all do it out of fear and to protect ourselves from the unknown. In my case, Rudy was not a person whom I chose to befriend. He didn't have the mental capacity to relate to others. I share his story now because he symbolized what we experience in our day-to-day lives. When we see or meet new people, we should hold our judgments, while at the same time protecting ourselves from those who may endanger us. Rudy's brain was scrambled like a two-dollar egg breakfast. It wasn't until I got close to him that I realized he was harmless and deserved understanding rather than fear and scorn.

I first saw Rudy in the rehab hospital's cafeteria. He usually had his shirt off for reasons that were unclear to me. It just seemed odd. I saw him about four or five times before I actually allowed myself to get close enough to meet him.

As he sat across from me at the dining room table, I thought it was tacky of him to eat with his shirt off. I had formed an opinion about him before I even met him. He seemed full of himself in an insulated, arrogant way. I could see that he thought he was what I would call a "badass." I wasn't sure what his history was, but he was admitted to rehab for a head injury. Several months before, he had found himself on the wrong end of his own baseball bat. He evidently had crossed the wrong person in some way. Early in the morning he was found in a vacant lot near where he lived in East Oakland, right in the heart of the urban warfare practiced by gangbangers, drug dealers, pimps, and those who get caught in the middle. His head had been beaten in with a baseball bat. The police later learned that the bat belonged to Rudy. He had come prepared to "take care" of someone only to be greeted with opponents who were better armed. Rudy had serious life-threatening head injuries: multiple skull fractures, a concussion, multiple lacerations and countless bruises. He was left for dead. To finish the job, his opponents shot him six times! Miraculously, he lived through the attack.

I learned his story and that his propensity to go without a shirt was his way of expressing his strength. He was a survivor, and he liked to show off his bullet wounds. It was only after this that I realized how I had prejudged this man who essentially was brain-damaged. He didn't look that way to me, but I was so busy thinking my own thoughts that I didn't take the time to be objective and look deeper into his situation.

During the recovery process, we go from compassion for self to compassion for others, and in doing so, we develop an evolved level of humanity. This evolution may be likened to what happens with a loss of hearing or the loss of sight. With a kind of emotional neuroplasticity we compensate for our loss by developing a higher vibration of awareness and in doing so, become more receptive and empathetic to the suffering and humanity of others. In short, we can better relate to them. Due to our strength in the face of disability or trauma, we can serve as role models to those either less or more fortunate.

ALLIES SEEMINGLY BAD OR GOOD.

Joni Eareckson Tada is a quadriplegic, a Christian motivational speaker, an author and a fine artist. She named the situation of being disabled, saying we are the players on the "Scale of Human Suffering." In her autobiography, *Joni*, Joni describes how a diving accident left her paralyzed, transforming her life forever, and her struggle to accept her disability and find renewed meaning in her life. In short, she says we serve to remind others that there is always someone who is worse off. And for us we see those who are more unfortunate than us and our heart fully goes out to them, thus enhancing our own humanity.

She is a role model in many ways. When I read her book there were many things that seemed to fit my situation. Like me, she is an artist. She paints with a brush in her mouth now and has refined that skill to a very high level. Her approach to healing is as an Evangelical Christian. She does missionary work, speaking to large audiences, inspiring and showing them she was lifted up and renewed by her religious and spiritual beliefs. That is where our similarities part. But my awareness of her came at a good time. It was a time when I was searching for truth, meaning and an understanding of what had happened to me. I was involved with a group of Christians at that time and was doing a Bible study called "Operation Timothy." I learned many great quotes from the Bible that lifted me up and gave me comfort, hope and peace. Here are a couple that were meaningful to me:

Proverbs 3:5-6
Trust in the Lord with all your heart and lean not on your own understanding; in all your ways submit to him, and he will make your paths straight.

Isaiah 40:31
But they that wait upon the Lord shall renew their strength; they shall mount up with wings, as eagles; they shall run, and not be weary; and they shall walk, and not faint.

The Operation Timothy course encouraged me on my path to recovery. As part of a group named the Christian Businessmen's Connection I helped coordinate Joni's appearance in Santa Cruz, California, at the Cocoanut Grove Ballroom near the Beach Boardwalk. The private conversation we had along with her wonderful speech about how she had been given her joy back when she found the Lord were a positive influence on me. Her experience and spirituality helped me come to terms with the loss of all the physical activities I used to enjoy. I am much more OK than I used to be. Step by step, I went deeper introspectively and analytically on my journey to self-acceptance. This can be a painful journey – sometimes taking a lifetime to achieve. But we must remind ourselves to adapt as best as we can and go on with our chins held as high as we can manage under the circumstances.

Regarding prejudging people keep this in mind. When we first see a person who seems off, we need to give them a little grace. When we learn to keep our jury out on people, we leave room for new information. We then allow this person to evolve in our opinion of them. In short, we allow them to redeem themselves before we condemn them.

Chapter 9

GURU ON A GURNEY:
Getting the Joy Back

Concentrate on things your disability doesn't prevent you doing well.
Don't regret the things it interferes with.
People won't have time for you if you are always angry and complaining.
—Stephen Hawking

Regaining your inner joy is a solo act. My advice is to start rebuilding it by having personal quiet time. Distance yourself from distractions like mindless television programs and indulge yourself in contemplation of your new situation. You can awaken to your inner joy. The seeds of higher consciousness germinate in the fertile ground of thoughtful introspection. Just to be able to sit with yourself quietly is a gift. It's surprisingly productive. Peace of mind and the resulting joy is the by-product of this inexpensive gift. You create the stillness in your life by taking time to be with and in yourself, not a half block down the road.

You will get a glimpse of what begins to make you feel better when you really start paying attention to what is driving your joy away. When your joy is kicked in the gut, this is the time for you to step into the adult mind and analyze who, or what thought did it, and why. Was this perpetrated or did your old reactive behavioral patterns cause it? Achievement of inner joy can be attained and I believe it is the ultimate quest and most profound goal. Isn't the most important achievement your happiness? A good look at what makes life joyful can be a step in defining the question of what makes us happy. Everything we choose is to get away from pain and pursue pleasure, unless we enjoy suffering.

One of my greatest joys as an artist is immersing myself in nature. I love how nature comes alive after I have been painting for a while. The same thing happens with people who see me painting quietly. Art provides a wonderful cross-cultural experience allowing me to penetrate deeper into different civilizations, affirming my belief that the family of man is one. From an unpopulated view of a tropical beach to the grinding streets of Manhattan, people are interested in the artist and his process of making art. My paintings are representative of my personal interpretation of where I am and are based on my feelings about the subject. A landscape may be loose if I am comfortable and the day is warm and breezy. If it is a painting of another culture, I may introduce more detail, like decorative pottery, to represent the nuances of that experience. It was luck to be born an artist - I have always been motivated to create.

Use what you have to re-claim something in yourself.

I believe that we are all creative in some way. Those of us who are artistic or musical are often able to suspend self-judgment long enough to maintain joy in the act of creation. If somehow you have lost your creative gift along the path of your life, you can find it now. It might be a different expression of your original creative path, but it can still give you the pleasure you once enjoyed. Search for and reclaim the enjoyable and playful aspect of your personal creativity. Think about what part of yourself you gave up when you were led to believe that you were not creative. Be mindful that we create for ourselves and the creative by-product is what we share with others. An act of creativity can be an act of literal re-creation.

Your inner life can be enhanced by taking your inner ideas and transforming them into reality. The process can give you some peace and take your focus off your injury. You may have powerful feelings that can be creatively put into words that may help you heal. Any creative action will turn undermining forces into a positive mind-set and generate energy in you.

Your creative act will yield a moment when disorder gives way to order and something new emerges. Your creative capacity can make you feel that life is worth living.

Consider the difference of creativity versus artistic ability. We are all born with creativity but not necessarily artistic ability. This creativity is with us for our whole life and each gift of creativity is unique from person to person. Creativity comes into play with problem solving. It is the mother of invention where we search for alternatives. You can be creative without artistic ability. If you have artistic ability and are creative then your artwork will be highly personal and unique. It is important to understand the distinction between the two. Your creativity can be used in many ways and is a force that is enriching and healing spiritually. Embrace your creativity as it will make a positive change in you.

In the rehab hospital I painted with a brush in my mouth for months. I had creativity and artistic ability. It was interesting to see my artwork progress. Perhaps you may consider a creative act of some type if you don't have artistic ability. There are many ways to express creativity without using your hands. Can you tell a good story? What about poetry, lyrics or invention? I played the harmonica sometimes with a hands free holder.

If you do this creative work, do it to please yourself. Suspend all judgment and keep the "play" aspect alive in the process. Your personal creativity and style will show through in all you do. It will emerge and please you. Sharing your creativity can be shared later or not at all, it is your call. Whatever you have in mind creatively, bring it into the world.

Creativity is something that might serve as a thread to string beads of small pleasures on. It will be uniquely yours, and when seen or experienced by others will give you the ability to share the happiness you have created for yourself. When I was able to paint again, it was very fulfilling. It was not great art at first, but it was authentic and expressive which is the foundation of great art. As you continue to create, it will gain mass and momentum and pull you forward. Artistry and creativity, like happiness, are "inside jobs." Please yourself. It's OK.

After my paralysis, the first artwork that I did was in the Occupational Therapy Department in Ralph K. Davies in San Francisco. At the time, I was still a quadriplegic. I sat up as best I could by being strapped into a wheelchair and was wheeled up to an easel with a large sheet of paper. My therapist would mix up some paints and load the brush for me, and then stick the brush handle into my mouth. I did more than a hundred paintings and drawings with my mouth during the period I was an inpatient. I experienced the refinement of the marks I made, and seeing my efforts rewarded with improvement encouraged me. At first, my drawings and paintings were very basic, but with time and practice I was able to express what I wanted. This therapeutic activity bolstered my belief that I could do art again. As I progressed, I recognized more and more of my personal style in the art I was creating. It looked like I had done it. I had reclaimed a fundamental part of myself through my art.

FEAR OF INADEQUACY, AND NOT BEING ENOUGH FOR OTHERS.

Own it right now that your disability is not your fault, and if it is, that there is nothing that you can do about it now, anyway. That was then and this is now. Take this opportunity to discover yourself and the integrity that is yours. Spend some time discovering what feels good about being you. What is the irreducible element of your identity, without which you would no longer be the person you believe yourself to be? Spend some time thinking about what your real interests are and then follow them. Don't be afraid to spend time with yourself, get comfortable with yourself, by yourself. Do what feels good to do and brings you some type of joy. If you start slowly and treat spending time with yourself as an exercise, these moments will result in the process of self-discovery and re-creation. As you get into the process of doing what feels right to you, you will not need to seek the approval of others, but will find that the authenticity of what you do will indeed yield your own self approval: a profound concept. It will come on its own. You will be surprised because you will find that outside approval and stimulation is not needed. You will have given approval to yourself and that will be the best self-affirmation you can get. This is how I healed my feelings of inadequacy in the face of my disability.

BANISH THE FEELING OF BEING UNWORTHY.

When I was finally emotionally healed, I found that I no longer needed to seek affection. I still can picture myself, as a boy in the kitchen helping my Mom, hoping to be recognized as a good kid. This early behavior set up a pattern in my life, one of seeking recognition, rather that finding self-fulfillment in simply being helpful. Self-worth seemed to come on its own in direct proportion to my degree of self-discovery and self-acceptance. I discovered that my insecurities were a product of falling short of the needs of my insatiable ego. The more I learned about what the ego is, the more I could do battle with it. Ego is the voice that says "I am not enough" and that "there is not enough to go around for all." I learned when I operated from my ego, that I lost my focus and balance. I learned that all my insecurities are the stuff that my ego thrives on. My ego's erroneous needs propelled me into dysfunction. I learned that I had created a false self. This self-protecting being that my ego created was "Prince Edward." He was charming, false, selfish, superficial and indifferent to the needs of others. Essentially this false self was created to project a persona that my ego thought would be acceptable. Ultimately, I found that the authentic plain old me, warts and all, was much more acceptable, interesting and lovable to others. What a relief.

ENGAGE YOUR GOOD QUALITIES.

For some reason, as a kid, I got it in my head that I was a bad boy. I was a bright, creative, energetic kid with few boundaries. I think my conclusion was a product of child rearing when the distinction between the action versus the person acting was not made clear to me. When my parents said, "you are a bad boy for doing that" rather than "that was a bad thing to do", it had a profound effect on the formation of my self-concept. Not separating the doer from the deed was the way kids were raised back then.

As a kid, I often acted out and was taken out of parochial school and put into public school where I also had problems. I developed a strong sense of negative self-worth as a result. But this was the way kids were raised then, and I have now let go of what was done to me, as well as how it affected my self-perception in the name of discipline and guidance. Whatever behaviors I chose in those days evidently were what I needed at the time to fill my needs. As a child I was self-directed and not sheepish. As my childhood friend Philip J. Wagner said, "Well, Ed was always a goat, not a sheep."

WORK TOWARD HAPPINESS.

The new reality of your disability is a great opportunity to examine the context of your life and see if it is what works. What I mean is to look at your life before, and ask yourself if you were happy. If not, what are the factors or who are the individuals who are depriving you of having peace of mind? What is it that is blocking your effort to gain strength, self-esteem, and physical and psychological well being? Recognize, too, that some things can not be changed. That's OK, you are different now; your experience has given you a pass to judge for yourself what is best for you. This growth is about you and no one else. Do you choose fierce independence, cooperative balance, or do you choose to be passively dependent?

I had a friend who knew he wasn't happy in his marriage, but stayed in his struggling marital relationship for an additional five years for the sake of his sons. It would have been better for them if he had stepped up and cut all of their losses. It was a bad choice to hang in there in a half-hearted way, as ultimately they divorced, anyway, and everyone was damaged in the process. The point is that we always have thresholds, and we all have choices.

All choices are legitimate, depending on your needs and what you can comfortably live with. Separate yourself by taking time with yourself. You can call it prayer or meditation. Whatever your method, that time should be the opposite of struggle in that you will clear your mind of all clutter and simplify your personal vision of your new self.

Take a minute to visualize a joy-filled moment you have experienced. It might be a moment you shared with someone you care for, or it may be the attainment of a particular goal you worked to achieve. Just hold your vision and thought, while I share another personal joy with you.

When I was thirteen I wanted a new bike, and I wanted it badly. I was consumed with it to the extent that I carried a picture of it with me for months. To earn money for the bike, I took a job at Bud's Used Furniture and Appliance Store in the Chinatown of Santa Cruz. My job was to clean stoves and refrigerators as well as to strip and sand furniture. It was hard work, and the refrigerators were the worst … literally disgusting. My distracting thoughts of friends playing ball, enjoying the nice weather outside, and having fun were a constant challenge to me. I wanted to be with my friends, but instead I took out the photo and kept my goal of a new bike literally in my mind. Each time I got paid, I walked to the bike shop, looked at the new bikes and gave them all my earnings. Again, another goal-oriented choice. I followed this pattern until I got my new bike. What joy. The bike was not the true gift in my case, rather it was the lesson that I could work toward a goal, make positive choices and feel really good about myself for what I had accomplished. Enjoying the new bike and the admiration of my friends was the cherry on top.

Now, the thought you are holding can tell you something about yourself, and what your needs are for happiness. What led to this positive joyful feeling? You may remember the feeling clearly and recognize that good choices lead to good things, and bad ones lead to negative things, or nothing at all and no joy.

Although yours is a singular journey, it is important to share with safe people like a therapist who can help give you a game plan and suggest new coping mechanisms. Or, share problems with a loved one who honestly cares for your wellbeing. As you creatively visualize how things can change to improve your progress, you can set goals and ask for helpful strategies to accomplish them without damaging others or yourself. After I learned how to write again, I used three by five cards while in therapy to take notes and it really helped me. They were like a deck of cards with situations, solutions, reminders and more. If there is no way for you to physically take notes, you are within your rights to ask for some of these thoughts to be written down for you. Seeing your thoughts and feelings in writing will help clarify them for you. Be positive about this process to find the unknown treasures that have been deposited in your subconscious by virtue of your losses and suffering. It is in there to be revealed as strength and wisdom for your future.

HOLD ON TO YOUR JOY-FILLED MOMENTS.

Joy and happiness is inside of you in a box with golden hinges. On the lock, the words "Mindful Choices," are inscribed. The more often you unlock "Mindful Choices", use it and add examples to it, the bigger and stronger it will grow and it will help you to cultivate your happiness.

WHY NOT TRY THIS? IT HELPED ME.

Sit some place comfortable where you will not be disturbed for a while. If you need to ask not to be disturbed, do so. Make this your time.

- As you sit quietly, breathe regularly with a bit more emphasis as you inhale.

- Feel the peace come over you as you continue to breathe in an even and comfortable rhythm.

- Visualize a small box with a golden keyhole and hinges. You have in your imaginary hand a decorative antique gold key.

- Imagine the small box has a plaque with engraved words in elegant script lettering which says "Mindful choices."

- Think of a time you made a positive conscious choice that empowered you. Your choice may be as simple as a time you said "no" when you needed to.

- Imagine grasping the key, unlock the lid, place the example "no" in the box and name it. It could be named "Bob" representing a personally empowering moment.

- Take the time you need. Imagine the box filled with good and positive power, all empowering moments in your life.

- Think about the choice you need to make. Sit with the choice you will make when a situation arises that will call for you to be non-reactive, rational and calm.

- Know the box is calming, empowering, is in your heart and will always be with you. You always have the key. Lock your box and return it to your heart.

- Breathe deeply like a sigh and own that you have peace and it is yours alone. Smile as you open your eyes knowing that you have chosen to engage life positively.

PAUSE BEFORE CHOICES.

I got a phone call from a person who had always been troublesome. I mean the kind of person who always seemed to have some drama they had brought upon themselves, and who is so exhausting to be around that I could hardly wait to get away from her. This person asked if we could get together for a visit. As soon as I heard her voice, it filled me with dread. The idea of reconnecting with this person was not something I wanted to do. I knew that I would be drawn into this person's drama and dysfunction. Against my better judgment, I agreed to meet. But immediately after hanging up the phone, I began to feel worse and worse about the fact that I had agreed to meet her. I knew it was more than just a meeting; because of her personality, I was essentially opening a door to chaos and upset. I decided to cancel. I called her back and said that I had changed my mind and would not meet her. I was definitive about it and she had no choice but to accept my decision. When I hung up, I enjoyed a sigh of relief. It was an example of me taking care of myself. It was a victorious experience. I could add the experience to my box of mindful choices and could draw strength from it later.

TAKE A MINUTE AND VISUALIZE BEING JOY FILLED.

There's a little thing I do from time to time that gets me in touch with myself and makes me happy: I visualize being filled with joy. I first started doing this after I had been in the hospital for months and bed baths were the only way I was kept clean. A bowl of warm soapy water and a sponge worked fine to keep me feeling clean and comfortable. A lotion called Lubriderm was used to keep my skin from getting dry and cracked, which could lead to painful bedsores. When it was time for a shampoo, the nurse would get a large black plastic trash bag, put it under my head and shoulders and secure it to the bed. Then she would take warm water and dampen my hair, shampoo it and rinse it with a pitcher of warm water. The water would be caught in the plastic bag then gathered up after putting my head in a towel.

Then one day I was given my first real shower on a shower gurney which is a tight mesh net stretched over a gurney-like structure with wheels, primarily used for moving paraplegics and quadriplegics. After months of bed baths, the purifying water running all over my body and the warmth everywhere felt so extraordinary, it is hard to describe! Following the shower, which I tried to prolong as long as possible, the nurse transferred me into a wheelchair. She wrapped me in a thick white cotton bath blanket with a bath towel around my head, Hindu style.

Bathing was such a wonderful experience that I was overflowing with happiness and joy. It was amazing how the simple pleasure of a shower could bring me such bliss. I felt deeply cleansed. I wanted to share my good feeling with anyone I could, so I begged the nurse to please wheel me in to visit some of my unfortunate hospital mates and pretend that I was a guru. I spoke with an accent; I had always loved the wisdom of the East and delighted in the lyrical accent of Indians speaking English as a second language. The sound was one of hope and faith as well as a sense of wellbeing. I was received as a farcical "holy man" and honestly found that my blessings momentarily healed both myself and the spirit of those with whom I visited. The more they would engage and role-play with me, the better it was for all. I was bringing happiness to others and myself at the same time. My mantra for them was, "The secret to happiness is to be happy."

It was a game of make believe that evolved from a need to break out of my mental straitjacket caused by my total physical paralysis. It sounds silly, but if you look at the underpinnings of the mind, you can see that the technique will work. Still, it was impossible for certain patients to play this silly game. I used my judgment so as not to overstep and intrude on those who were suffering acutely. I visited patients who were my friends, ones who knew and liked me well enough to benefit from this positive little role-play.

If you are being thwarted in your mental progress over your disability by a negative viewpoint, you can break free from that into a newer and more positive one. You will prevail over your present traumatic situation by learning to view yourself and your dilemma through positive and brave eyes. Your goal must be to transcend your challenge.

Chapter 10

HONOR YOURSELF:

Feel Comfortable in Your Own Skin

Acceptance of what has happened is the first step
to overcoming the consequences of any misfortune.
—William James

E arly in my disability, I turned feeling sorry for myself into an art form. Being confined not only to a hospital bed, but to a body that had no response was a completely foreign experience. It was like double paralysis. And it was taking its toll on my mind as I tried to make some kind of sense out of my situation. I found myself trying out a multitude of personality coping styles and behaviors.

When first hospitalized, I didn't think I had any power at all. I was passive, willing to accept my lot as it related to the dictates of physicians and the responses of the hospital staff. I just went along with the flow. What else could I do? As a result, I went through periods of discreet personality changes. I started out as "the victim", then I became "the comedian," the "warrior of healing," the "accepting lost soul," and then finally, I came into my own new being with a sense of enlightenment and knowing. Over the course of many months, I had experienced and processed denial, bargaining, anger, sadness and acceptance. Most of this was conscious, some of it visceral or by osmosis by virtue of my context. It took me a long time to realize that what I needed to do was accept the death of my physiology as I had known it at least for the time being.

I have a made a successful transition into my new reality. It was incremental and conscious. That doesn't mean that I still don't occasionally look into a mirror and marvel at what has happened to me, or stop and recollect with tears the old pleasures now lost. But I have learned to love how I see myself now. In many ways, I'm a new, better version of who I was before. A key part of the healing process is embracing your new reality in order to believe in yourself again.

BELIEVE IN YOUR OWN WELLBEING.

During my own process toward the recovery of self, I was able to draw from a few experiences that had a positive effect on my self-outlook. For instance, I have been a member of the Rotary Club of Santa Cruz, California, for many years. We have events to raise money for local non-profit groups and those events usually involve an auction, dinner, dancing and entertainment of all sorts. At one event I recall Judy Nickelson, the wife of one of the members, asked me to dance. She was unrelenting, tall, quite attractive, and strong. She held me up and kept me from losing my balance as I attempted to dance with her — with one arm around her and the other grasping my Lofstrand crutch. My act of faith and the positive whim and persistence on her part was an ingredient that informed me that there was possibility beyond what I envisioned for myself. I was dancing, and I couldn't believe it!

Another building block experience that I had was also at a Rotary club auction. I wasn't much of a golfer, but before my disability I did like to play occasionally with buddies. I recall one of my friends asking me, after I had become disabled, if I would like to join them for a round of golf. He was mortified that he could make such an inappropriate social gaff. For me this was one of the most wonderful compliments that I had received since my disability. He had actually forgotten that I was disabled and could hardly stand or walk, and yet to him the bigger part of me prevailed and he wanted my company. I celebrated this deeply! Then, at another auction event later I bid on a round of golf, much to the shock and levity of the group in attendance. I gave the round of golf I had won to the person who had asked me to golf with him earlier. These things and other events helped me realize that personality can prevail over disability.

As I am getting older I find that I need to work harder at staying active and fit. It is challenge enough just to get around; but with the years ticking off, I have not only the disability to contend with, but also the prospect of going backward and having the aging process take a toll on me.

I was at my doctor's office waiting for my appointment time when an older fellow walked out of the examining room and up to the receptionist's desk to make another appointment and said, "It always makes me feel better when the doctor says 'make an appointment for a year from now.' I am encouraged he thinks I will still be around in a year!" What a great attitude.

I am going to do the best that I can, which is really all that anyone can do. But when you think of what that means, it really has impact. Doing the best that you can under any circumstances is profound, admirable and noteworthy, and it leads to feeling comfortable in one's own skin.

Disability, the Meaning.

When we make plans to do something we enjoy, we honor ourselves. If you decide that you want to do something, don't break a date with yourself. Don't stand yourself up. Remember friends don't cancel on friends. By honoring these commitments to yourself you can learn how to become your own best friend. Practice active self-regard instead of passive self-disregard. Be willing to do for yourself what you would want to do for someone who you really care a lot about. This strategy sounds like a simplistic tool, but it worked for me. Start a feel-good savings account and deposit each of your good feelings in it after you do something nice for yourself. Start to pick emotional low fruit rather than high fruit. Pick the things that fill you up whatever they are, as long as they make you feel better and are not self-destructive. You will know.

When I was a young boy I swam at a beautiful swimming hole in the Santa Cruz Mountains in a tiny little town called Brookdale. My family had been visiting this location for generations from about 1910 on. Eventually, my grandfather built a three bedroom redwood summer cabin there. The swimming hole is where I fell in love with my first girlfriend, Judy Ann, who attended Convent of the Sacred Heart in San Francisco. We were both thirteen. I recall those beautiful days floating in an old blue and white canvas covered canoe down the San Lorenzo River with Judy leaning against me. She was warm and innocently amorous. We watched the golden madrone leaves twirl past us on the smooth water mirroring the redwood trees above. Water-skeeters sculled across the cool clear water surface while trout and crayfish moved languidly below.

There were times through my healing journey when I would recall the high points of my life. The magical, the peak moments, the near celestial experiences that were of value and vivid in my memory. That place and time started to pop into my mind about the time I had regained a lot of mobility and was able to walk with crutches. As part of my emotional rehabilitation I thought it would be healing to go to the old swimming hole and do a painting of the location. I drove to Brookdale, unloaded my painting gear, "hiked" with great difficulty, with several trips and falls, down to the river's edge.

It was a beautiful summer day much like I remembered many years ago and it had not changed much. On the slope toward the river were vestiges of a large sand box made by my dad and his brothers, the diving area from old trestle pilings were there, as well as the tree where we had once made a rope swing.

After I had set up my watercolors and had been painting for a while, I heard footsteps coming down the path. It was a young lady in her early twenties ... and very lovely. I nodded to her and she smiled back. I continued painting as she spread out her towel and to my surprise lay down in the nude behind me.

A little later I heard some murmuring and another young lady had joined her. I kept painting, but couldn't resist taking a peek. Both ladies were sunbathing nude, a blonde and a brunette side by side. I painted the horizon line, the river, the trees, the reflections and a clear blue summer Brookdale sky. It was a perfect day. I continued to paint the structure of the narrow, old wooden bridge that crossed the San Lorenzo River. I was making good progress with my painting as the girls went into the shaded part of the river waist deep, it was beautiful, reminding me of the sensual painting by John Waterhouse, "Hylas and the Nymphs."

After a few moments I heard some kids talking loudly as they came down the path to the old swimming hole. Suddenly a Great Dane came bounding past the boys, charged over to me, and, stepping on my watercolor palette, began to drink the water from my water containers, slobbering all over my stuff, kicking up dirt. The dog, Buck, excitedly moved away and lifted his leg on the girl's picnic basket. With that not being enough he finished off my painting day by taking an elephantine dump no more than five feet from where I was sitting.

Even though recapturing a bliss-filled echo of my youth didn't happen that day – we can't go back to Shangri-La – I found that making time for doing simple and pleasing things helped me move up to higher, more satisfying and encouraging things, like higher emotional ground. I made time for myself to sit in a pleasant environment to paint or draw. Just being quiet helped me because it was time for myself. Some take that time and nurture their soul through prayer and meditation, some sit by a fire and pet their cat. The key ingredient that helped me emotionally was non-productive time, or "my time", a time of being and not doing. If this is too passive for you, figure out something as long as it is time for you to be with yourself and learn how to enjoy your singular company.

Call on the little kid inside you. He's still in there and could probably use a friend now that you are isolated in self-reconstruction. It is singular work that you alone will need to do. Remember what it was like to play alone as a kid. Dig those skills back up. They are still in there for you. The tools will feel surprisingly comfortable in your hand if you still have one. If not, you get my drift.

Try becoming invisible. It's very relaxing. You will find that you will leave your mental junk behind by witnessing yourself in your surroundings. View yourself as if you are in a play on stage. You can do this anywhere and it can be amusing. As part of this you can create your own protective bubble of self-love that cannot be penetrated. The degree of impenetrability depends solely upon you. This is a beginning exercise of your mind, and it is essential for your self-containment and mental healing.

By paying attention to our pain-filled feelings when we are around certain people, or our feelings when we even think of these people, it will provide us clues as to who we should keep out of our life. Right now this is about you and your reconstruction; you can re-admit people later when you are more together. If we can't keep them out, then we need to learn to witness what happens when we are around these people, then learn from it as if you are in survival camp. With practice we can develop the self-preservation skill of mindful non-reaction. It may be productive for you to see and take an inventory of your emotional investment in painful relationships. Pain can result from something as minor as a casual friend who makes unkind jokes about you when trying to be funny. Remember, friends are friendly. Mean spiritedness or the impolite behavior from others deserves a polite ignore. This response is like the response of a refined lady when she doesn't acknowledge an off-color remark.

I was having breakfast with three friends, one of whom I greatly admire. My revered friend was speaking to a particular point and was interrupted by the other two friends with a silly and distracting side conversation. They were insensitive to his earnest intent to share his extensive knowledge about the topic of the conversation. Rather than reacting negatively, he sat silently and motionless, with his hands in his lap until he was able to retake his platform gracefully. He politely ignored what he and I perceived as others being momentarily impolite.

Your reactionary behavior pattern will dissolve in direct proportion to how committed you are to becoming skilled at the practice of mindful non-reaction. This negative person will subsequently perceive you as an adult. Using this technique, you demonstrate that their negative behavior toward you no longer works to manipulate your feelings.

As long as you live, change must be embraced. There is no choice. You can think there is, but embracing change and doing so with your chosen positive attitude, will pull you through your present and future struggles. It does get easier and with each small victory, such as the experience of successfully dressing or feeding yourself after being completely paralyzed, you gain power. These successes all add up to a new and stronger you than before. This alone is worth fighting for; a chosen positive mind-set is your key. You cannot wimp out on yourself.

Chapter 11

THE ULTIMATE REDEFINITION:

Positivity, re-branding and the new self.

So many of our dreams at first seem impossible, then they seem improbable, and then, when we summon the will, they become inevitable.
—Christopher Reeve

Comedian Steve Martin once said, "It's hard not to be happy while playing the banjo. Just the sound of it makes one smile... Just imagine Richard Nixon walking along the beach playing the banjo!" There is humor in the absurd.

Norman Cousins healed himself from a deadly disease by watching the Marx Brothers, Laurel and Hardy, and other funny films. Just by losing himself in the present moment of humor, the release it gave him triggered a healing power. Your mind causes feeling. If you can control your mind, and you certainly can, then you can control your feelings and behavior.

Actors and actresses fall in love after making a film about love and romance. Acting supersedes our default mind-set and replaces it with a new reality. Our ego doesn't know the difference— it falls in love. My point is that with a little nudge, you can trick your ego into believing that you are happy. When I was in rehab I tried out this coping strategy. I was conscious of what I was doing, but I knew I needed a release of some kind or I was going to lose my entire mind. Acting happy helped me be happy.

ATTAIN A POSITIVE ATTITUDE.

I know this is old news, but the only thing you really can control in life is your attitude. Your attitude is like the breath you choose to take. If you unconsciously take shallow breath, you will feel weak, but if you consciously breathe in full, nourishing breaths, you'll feel instantly clear-headed and healthy. You can automatically dwell on the past and scorn fate, or you can mindfully gather up what you have left, claim your strength, and go forward with the belief that not only will you be OK, but you will prevail and perhaps even inspire others to see that one can have dignity in the face of a life-changing trial.

Your pride may have been annihilated by your disability, but your dignity is yours. Eddie Fung, a Chinese-American soldier who was a slave laborer during World War II, wrote of being in a Japanese prisoner of war camp. He was the only Chinese-American soldier to be captured by the Japanese in World War II and put to work on the Burma-Siam railroad made famous by the film *Bridge on the River Kwai*. In his moving memoir, Eddie recalls how his background as a Chinatown kid and Texas cowboy helped him endure 42 months of humiliation and cruelty, and how his experiences during the war shaped his later life. He reported the many humiliating and torturous events he endured for years. In the closing chapter of his book, *The Adventures of Eddie Fung*, he notes a key lesson he learned when in captivity: "I learned they could take my pride, but never my dignity."

Sure, there are moments when you won't be able to shake the sadness that you are changed forever, that you can't do everything you enjoyed before, that you look different, or now live a more restrictive lifestyle. Just like going through the death of a loved one, the loss of the ability to fully enjoy your body, be it a lost limb or the sight of your disfigured face in a mirror involves a long mourning process.

As a disabled person, I naturally use references to physical disability and trauma. Trauma includes the death of a loved one, divorce, physical loss, or any type of life changing event that is irrevocable. You can easily substitute the words of your choice for disabled and this information will work for you because this book is about loss, reorientation and recovery.

Your duty to yourself now and to your future happiness, no matter what your challenge, is not to get stuck in the anger stage of your emotional healing. This is personal work you will need to attend to, and the first step is to be aware of it, and now you are. Honestly, I often wonder if we can ever really fully heal from trauma, or if we either adjust and grow... or break from it.

LEARN TO LIKE YOUR NEW SELF.

What are you going to do? Are you going to hate your new self? That would be prejudicial — you don't even know your new self yet. Why not reinvent yourself? People change after trauma, either for better or worse. The change will be for the worse if you don't pay attention to your feelings about yourself and your new coping skills. I thought that once I got my life together again I would become a person who would be tough and disciplined to the core. But actually that didn't happen. I did learn compassion and the value of caring for others and being more flexible. What is interesting about redefining yourself after a trauma is that it is completely up to you how you choose to relate and navigate in and through life. Change may happen to you uncontrollably on the physical level, but on an emotional and spiritual level you are in complete control of your state of being. You need to own this wisdom and put it into practice. Keep it in mind as you grow through this.

Now you have the choice to go forward on a path of spiritual growth or be defeated by self-loathing and pity. You can look at your new disability as a battle scar and a medal of honor and courage, or you can look backwards to try to reclaim a past version of yourself as the only measure of your worth, and become frustrated, angry and toxic. As hard as it seems at first, look at your disability as an opportunity. Maybe you are not ready to do the work and should shelve this book for a few months. When you are feeling like your spirit is against the wall, you can pick it up and read about how those who have gone before you, after they lost who they were, have been able to transform into the kind of people who others like to be around and are inspired by. In many ways you have been chosen to do this work by fate or whatever you wish to call it. I have said many times about my own experience that on the stage of life I have been given the roles of the guy in the wheelchair, and now the guy with the crutch. If you can get to the point where you accept yourself in the present moment, you will be bigger than your disability and people will not even notice it. You can reinvent yourself. This is a fact of life.

REBRAND YOUR PERSONALITY, BUILD A MORE ACCURATE PERSONAL VIEW.

It was crucial for me to rebrand my self after my disability because now I was a new person. One method I used to help me get an understanding of my personality and self-concept was to make a list of all the traits that I do not posses, all the things that I am not. It seems it is natural for us to determine what we are not more easily than what we are. I listed things like impatient, greedy, rude, mean spirited, stingy, pushy, judgmental and other negative traits. Once I had that list, in a thesaurus I looked up all the antonyms for those words until I found one that I felt best fit me. For the word "stingy" I selected the word "generous." I could say and believe that one of my personal attributes was being "generous." I did this with all the words revealing a profile of my positive and defining attributes.

The next step was to imagine an image of an old fashioned roll top desk with many "pigeon holes" for filing items. My mental task was to label these individual holes with a positive trait, like "generous," etc. Once I had named the pigeon holes with all the words for my good traits. The next step was "ownership work." Now I had a place for positive traits to be placed and saved. When another person or myself said that I was fair, or kind, or generous or another distinguishing positive trait I could file it and make it my own rather than blithely dismissing it.

This metaphor worked for me as now I had a place for positive characteristics to land and be held. I paid attention so I could field and file these quality traits and begin to see and appreciate the consistency in my positive behaviors and way of being. I found that this technique of fielding and filing would interrupt my internal voice of negative judgment. The way I previously had thought myself began to get weaker as my self-concept was systematically reoriented to a stronger, encouraging and positive self-view. As I fielded, filed and owned my good qualities they pushed aside my previous inaccurate version of my self. This method helped me grow an accurate personal view of my new self. It did not take long to own the positive behavioral traits that make up who I really am. Now I can fully inhabit my real self.

HOW YOU PERCEIVE YOURSELF WILL DETERMINE HOW OTHERS SEE YOU.

Are you aware that people treat you the way you train them? Of course, they will first treat you as they wish based on their initial perception of you. Often this take on you is relative to that individual's past experience with people who may have similar physical characteristics to you. For example, if in grade school a redhead kid beat you up, then in the future when you meet a redheaded person, your perception of that person will be viscerally negative. If one allows this prejudice to take over, one limits oneself to never having redheaded friends based on a childhood memory.

If you stop and think for a minute about this phenomenon, you can see how it is only human to default to this type of lower cerebral functioning.

For the most part people have preconceived impressions of disabled, disfigured and traumatized individuals. In my personal experience, people often think people in wheelchairs are mentally diminished for some reason. Those whom the individual perceives as different create fear, because there is some element of the unknown, or the "other." That's human nature. Fortunately for you, this may work in your favor. If you are aware that this is an honest human imperfection, based on rather primitive mental functioning, it is easier to not react and be hurt. These individuals just don't know you yet. You can get past this initial obstacle, and you can make plenty of friends. In other words, it is not about you. Furthermore, if someone is too put off by the residue and imprint of your trauma, they might not be worth having as a friend.

LABEL YOURSELF.

For many years I have made a career as a marketing consultant and designer, studying businesses and developing brand identities for them. I can often see problems where the owner of the company is blind to the gap between the quality of their product or service and its presentation to market with appropriate, memorable identification and packaging. The most typical example is a company that has a good product but the packaging does not represent the contents. The appearance belies the content. It may be a good wine, but the label is off-putting and not memorable, and says nothing about the quality. This is a lot like when you meet a person and they completely surprise you with their depth of character, intelligence and uniqueness. We are dealing with your content as a human being, and your new packaging can tell the story of your courageous, unique and victorious character.

Brand identity is used in business for products and may be used for people as well. When a person starts a new business, or has fought their way through brutal company politics, they can be successful by virtue of branding themselves as the type of person who is courageous, can be relied upon, and has integrity and vision. It is important to take credit for your accomplishments, growth, vision, lessons learned, and talent.

There are three common myths about personal branding that are applicable to your present situation when it comes to making the adjustment to greet the world.

The first myth is that if the product (person) is good enough, then the customer (other person) will come. In our case, we need to engage the public boldly and make the statement about our contents. If you sit quietly you will be prejudged as being slow or defective, so now you need to learn to be engaging. You must show your contents – how you have prevailed over the challenge – and claim your victory in the new way you represent yourself.

The second myth is "marketing is a dirty business." It is not. It is a fact of life in business as well as in the personal realm. This means that you take a good objective look at yourself and claim the profound lessons you have learned and share them with others. Now you may let them know what you went through and can share your insights about personal strengths that you didn't even know you had until your back was up against the wall. You can be a hero even to yourself if you claim it. Actually it is almost like others want you to do this so they can have someone to admire. You can label yourself in an authentic, consistent and memorable way that you can be proud of. Start speaking to your content; it is rare that people go through what you have been going through and they want to know about your strength and success.

The third myth is that we cannot control what others think. Not true.

You can present yourself so that others will think differently and positively about you. You are a product of your experience. You have figured out who you are, what you stand for, and why you are different from anyone else. You can communicate your value and your uniqueness. You can tell your story better than anyone else, with more passion, more believability and without apology. You will discover that there is strength and clarity in you that you didn't know of. You can claim your rightful place among those who have examined themselves deeply and honestly, and contemplated how they fit into the world at large, how they feel about that, and finally how they can live with authority. Your story is yours to tell and no one else's.

BE EXTROVERTED.

Only you can decide when you will "come out" after healing your wounds. It's up to you to decide when to get out of your comfort zone. Meeting new people is a good place to start. New people don't know who or what you were before this present moment and that is a powerful way to break out of the mental jail you may find yourself in. It may be an interesting exercise for you to see how you fare with no past in the mind of this new friend. In her book about cancer, *It's Always Something,* comedienne Gilda Radner introduces herself to an old friend by saying, "Hi, I used to be Gilda Radner!" In that moment she finds strength and humor in the immutable fact that her life, identity and being have been forever changed. She showed courage in the face of certain death and lightened her load and the load of those around her by finding sardonic humor in her terminal condition. In my case, I'd say that most people who are my friends like me more after my disability than before.

EPILOGUE:

Embrace your inner magic.

Others may call what you do heroic. It really boils down to your choice about how to deal with your current situation and your future. So perhaps the most heroic action is the choice to make the best of your situation. We either adjust to our new circumstances or we don't. If we do make an adjustment and reinvent our self-images within our new world, then survival becomes much easier. You must have vision, learn, create, dream, and feel; you must innovate a new self for a new life. If we don't adapt, we will live in the past, measuring our new world by our old one. For instance, you can dwell on getting fired, or you can embrace the change and all it may offer in terms of potential. What is truly heroic is your decision to pivot, to change, and to embrace your struggle and the unknown ancillary gifts it may bestow upon you. You must choose to pick up the remaining pieces of your life and go forward to build a new one. If you don't go forward positively, you will be going backward negatively. A positive attitude is what will make you a success because, as you know, a big part of success in life is how you choose to deal with your emotional, psychological, physical or any other challenge.

You can choose to prevail, or you can choose to spiral downward. This is largely a spiritual battle. How do you keep your spirits up? You choose to, you don't give up; you don't become a shadow of your old self, but a newer and stronger revision of yourself. Use the skills set out for us by the visionary innovators of the world, and be brave. Use your life situation as an opportunity to re-label your new and revised character. Use all the lessons you have learned during your unique predicament. Your life experiences will give you the strength. The unique experiences that only you have lived through and the introspective and existential moments of near psychic annihilation that you own now are your power source and uniquely yours alone.

As a challenged person, you may think that you are different and don't fit in. Physically you may be different, but beyond that, on the big plus side, your mind and spirit are different now, too. You can change your perspective. Rather than thinking about how to fit in, you can view this as an opportunity to figure out if you really do want to fit in, after all.

You are forced to have a deeper human experience now and will live life more deeply than others in many ways. When you realize that you have consciously met death in a more full way than others who just flirt with the abstract concept of non-being by, for instance, bungee jumping, your amplified existential awareness will cause you to think and feel differently about life.

In many ways when we talk about death it is as a grand final conclusion. Yet it actually has many gradients. More than death, I would like to address the concept of body death and mind death. The inability to grasp change and embrace it positively is what causes disabled people to be unhappy. If we cling to our pre-disabled image, we will spend the balance of our days in this miraculous plane comparing ourselves to our past self. To adjust to your new reality you will need to release your former self-image. Have you ever considered the richness of your experience, and how it has already made, or will make, your life more intense and real? Think of all the people who you know who are really just sleepwalking through life.

By virtue of your challenges and your ability to persevere and conquer, you are stronger and will live a grand and more authentic life. A by-product of this is the development of your courage and compassion. You will have, or already have, courage to be strong and continue on when others would quit. Believe me, this could be something as simple as buttoning a shirt!

BE STRONG.

I recall an afternoon about ten years ago when I was getting dressed for a formal fund raising dinner and auction. I knew I needed to give myself plenty of time to get ready so I started around three that afternoon. I wanted to arrive around six in the evening for cocktails and conversation with friends. I pulled all my clothes together: tuxedo, starched tux shirt, cuff links, studs, cummerbund, bow tie, and some crafted dress shoes I bought in Italy when I had a different life. I showered, shaved, and sat on the bed with all clothes laid out for easy access. I put on underwear, socks and started with my tux shirt. I slipped it on and tried to insert the studs into the holes on the front of the pleated shirt bib, but the shirt was so heavily starched that it was difficult to insert studs.

When I first re-learned to button buttons in rehab, I started with large plastic buttons about an inch and a quarter diameter because my fingers were weak and deformed with little pinching ability. Now I was attempting to deal with small slippery gold and onyx studs. I tried and tried to get the studs into the little slots and finally got one into the slot and attempted to bring the other half of the shirtfront into position so that I could attach it. As much as I tried it was not going to happen. I tried again using a button hook to enlarge the starchy slot so the stud would more easily slip into position. That did not work either. Now I had spent an hour just trying to get my shirt buttoned and I still had not succeeded. I decided to take the shirt off and lay it out flat on my bed and try it that way. I was finding the studs too slippery and the shirt too starchy to succeed. I regrouped as my patience was being sorely tested by these failed attempts.

I had learned patience and persistence in the rehab hospital. To succeed you take the end result out of the equation and focus on the task at hand. I sat with the problem for a while and decided to try to use needle nose pliers that I had in my home office. They were small and spring loaded so they were easy to use with my limited hands. One by one I successfully loaded all the studs but the top collar button, and left it open. I then slipped the shirt on over my head, messing up my hair, but happy to have a buttoned shirt. I used the button hook on the top button and buttoned it. I had one stud missing and I put it in my pocket, deciding that I would just ask someone to quickly do it for me.

The next step was to put in my cuff links. Think about putting a cuff link on with one hand and the dexterity it takes even with your dominant hand! I reamed out the slots in the heavily starched French cuffs, opening them so I could more easily insert the cuff link and then snap the bar on it to secure the cuff. Now I had been working at my shirt project for an hour and forty-five minutes. Half way through my first cuff and still holding my patience, trying not to give up, not be discouraged, persevering to victory over my challenging garb, I got my cuff links in by sheer patience and determination. I visualized how I was going to do it and tried and retried until I succeeded. I had used up two and a half hours just trying to get my shirt on. I was feeling dizzy from my effort and the extent I had controlled my emotions.

I was able to get the rest of my tux on, found that the nice shoes would accommodate my plastic foot braces and I re-brushed my hair. I was about fifteen minutes late and ready to see my friends. I was not going to be beat down by a button or lack of determination. My friends were glad to see me; however, they did not know I had been doing battle with my shirt for hours. They say that a woman wearing beautiful lingerie feels a sense of confidence and satisfaction even if it cannot be seen. In my case, the secret story no one knew was winning my battle with my shirt. It gave me satisfaction and power. There is a general strength that I gained from my repeated commitment to prevailing over my limitations. When I got home that evening I delighted in ripping my shirt off, swearing to never wear a tuxedo shirt again unless I hired a valet!

Ultimately you will prevail, and with this you will earn patience and respect for yourself. Own your persistence and effort consciously, physically, and give yourself credit for having fortitude. The compassion you give to yourself is usually given to others because you learned and earned a deeper understanding of human failure. It is crucial that you give compassion to yourself because you have earned it. This process is much like love, forgiveness, and self-respect, in that you present it to yourself as a gift. By doing this, you realize that you are not just fully human, but in some ways super human. Though sometimes it is hard to believe, you deserve credit! Choose to live with dignity, and remember some of the things I have shared with you about self-love. You deserve no less than your highest goal. And remember, we get what we settle for. Your basic sense of self and dignity are infallible. Realize that, and own it.

I wish you luck and good fortune, as this is the hardest and most rewarding work that you will ever do.

You are up to you.

APPENDIX:

INSIGHTS FOR YOUR JOURNEY.

These insights are a way to shortcut complex issues in a light weight package, like a fortune-cookie-ism or a haiku. These insights mean something to me because they are answers to my personal questions, but I offer them here to perhaps help you on your path to understanding, growth, adaptation and serenity.

And if insights come to you, please note them and send them to me.

THOUGHT ON CLARITY
Get it... please.

THOUGHT ON HEALING
To fully heal ourselves,
we must fully bury that part of us which is dead.

THOUGHTS ON HAPPINESS
The real joys in life may be intangible.

THOUGHT ON TRAGEDY
The irrevocable loss, the deadening pain,
the unanswerable question of a child's senseless death.

THOUGHT ON UNCERTAINTY
Every problem has an answer,
and that answer resides in defining the problem.

THOUGHT ON FAILURE
I had dreams, I will dream again.

THOUGHT ON SERENITY
So much power wasted on doubt.

THOUGHT ON CONTENTMENT
Bring back a childlike sense of well-being.

THOUGHT ON SELF-AWARENESS
I surprise myself with my truth.

THOUGHT ON GROWTH
Raise your own vibration.

THOUGHT ON COURAGE
I am a hard act to follow, even for myself.

THOUGHT ON PEACE
If you want to arrive at peace, don't pack your ego.

THOUGHT ON PRETENSE
Use until empty, discard container, no refills.

THOUGHT ON LIFE
My life is a sacred text.

THOUGHT ON TRUST
Trust is a door to love, a window to the self,
a tribute to strength and honor.

THOUGHT ON ENDINGS
Every door closed on me opens to another.

THOUGHT ON LOVE
The rarest of commodities, hard to find, harder to keep.

THOUGHT ON SUFFERING
It's a kind of celestial triage; God will get around to you.

THOUGHT ON HAPPINESS
The key to happiness is to be happy.

THOUGHT ON LIFE
I'll have a double scoop of life on a sugar cone, please.

THOUGHT ON PASSION
There may be no logic.

THOUGHT ON FATE
Why me? Why not me?

THOUGHT ON INNER VISION
You may be blind for the journey inward.

THOUGHT ON SUFFERING
Someone has it worse than you,
be thankful you are not on their path.

THOUGHT ON HAPPINESS
Gratitude, the best anti-depressant I can think of.

THOUGHT ON TIME
Youth is hormonal, aging cerebral,
everything in between a gradient.

THOUGHT ON MEANING
Mine is to reason why, not to blindly do and die.

THOUGHT ON DISINTEGRATION
When energy moves out through you.

THOUGHT ON HEALING
I release the past in a profound and liberating belch.

THOUGHT ON STRENGTH
I lock out the thief of fear, doubt and resentment.
I hold like a treasure my joy, vision and love.

THOUGHT ON HEALING
I have survived another loss. It is OK. I will be well.

THOUGHT ON BLISS
When passion and desire merge.

THOUGHT ON SELF
I claim my sanity, I own my serenity.

THOUGHT ON POWER
Mind your own power.

THOUGHT ON MATERIAL
Never ask for anything you wouldn't be willing to give away.

THOUGHT ON LIFE
Life may be a joke, but I get it.

THOUGHT ON RELEASE
Breathe, breathe, breathe. It's OK.

THOUGHT ON ACCEPTANCE
If we drive away love, we cannot cry out in loneliness.

THOUGHT ON SELF
Maintain a sense of wellbeing,
honor your higher nature and self worth.

THOUGHT ON SELF
I peruse and appreciate my life as a non-objective work of art.

THOUGHT ON TIME
Save some time, accelerate the inevitable.

A sampler of poetry.

These are from my book *In Memoriam Innocentium*, poems of love, loss, healing, inspiration, humor, joy and gratitude.

WHEELCHAIR

A quiet boy asked of my legs.
He came up still and near.
Uncomfortable mother scolded him,
he was compassionate, and so clear.

THE JOY OF GETTING OUT.

Leaning back, looking out.
I'm going for a ride.
this present path that I am on
has vaporized my pride.

I have a blue adapted van
for where I want to go.
My dependency it is major,
so I keep expectations low.

Into a blue parking zone
smoothly do we glide.
Driver friend she cares for me,
as into the world we ride.

Bracket screwed into my head.
It's for my fusion's sake.
Guards against jolts and such
my neck not to re-break.

Locked in like an astronaut,
my arms are tied down too.
The situation's clearly mine,
but as well it could be you.

I've had a tracheotomy
and I can't say a thing
or write notes, or code to you.
It's all so limiting.

Soon she will be feeding me.
It comes in through a tube
a milk shake of vanilla.
At last, it's normal food.

Patiently she holds it up
so in me it will drain.
I gulp at it the best I can,
trying not to freeze my brain.

I never killed an ant or flea,
and wonder why I'm here.
Perhaps my role is to awaken those
who are sleeping and not so clear.

When I move I'm careful too,
the planning and the setting.
Seldom do I go outside,
but nature not forgetting.

We stop and she unlocks me,
will lower down the ramp.
My van is all fixed up for me.
It keeps me on the map.

I am waiting in my chair,
now it's time to move.
So much anticipation,
countless weeks inside a room.

So long inside the hospital
I did reside foreboding,
sleeping not for nights on end,
kept wide awake by coding.

On the lift I'm teetering,
the lift it goes down lower.
This wheelchair is a part of me,
a gardener's well-used mower.

Chair switched on, I lurch ahead
to a spot of warmth and sun.
The air is fresh and noisy.
I am out doors, I'm one!

I drive my chair by solenoids,
my muscles they replace.
Now pleasantly I park myself
with sunshine on my face.

A squirrel has befriended me
because I am so still.
Closer and closer he comes to me,
like for peanuts on a sill.

Pigeons join the party
iridescent and so shiny.
Then tiny hatches come,
and finches landing shyly.

Unfolding in activity
and comfortably exciting,
happening when we're still,
quiet, reposed, inviting.

It is a natural party
when everything is still.
It's naturally so healing.
It's Mother Nature's pill.

SQUEAKY

Taking time to contemplate,
I sit parked inside my car.
The sound of bottles clinking
at a recycling bin not far.

Eyes are closed and sounds come up,
like various cars when passing,
no sounds of birds, or humankind,
only unnatural sounds harassing.

No, it seems that I am wrong.
I can hear some chirping birds,
a squeaky, rattling shopping cart,
a din not previously heard.

Opening one eye, I see birds in flight
soundless as they glide,
closer squeaks the shopping cart,
all belongings packed inside.

I close my eyes, breathe in the air,
it's clear and cool and fresh.
I breathe it in and calm myself,
as squeaks and clatter enmesh.

The cart is getting closer now,
the glass bottles are still breaking
an avalanche of "Miller Time"
accompany this break I'm taking.

Again, I open up my eyes,
I'm the goal of Squeaky's path,
as the cart comes up to me,
compassion displaces wrath.

I see the wounds of homelessness,
no trace of warmth or grace,
authentically so pitiful,
and beyond mankind's embrace.

Opening up to speak to me,
words rasp through missing teeth,
his dirty clothes and blanket,
society hath bequeathed.

Of course I give him money.
Squeaky needs some food to eat.
No part of me will refuse this,
looking down at crusty feet.

In my life I've had much help
from those I dearly loved,
also, help from therapists
and ones who gently shoved.

Saying no to eyes in need
is unforgiving, and sinful
if we realize all we have,
grace given by the bin full.

Born not of simple mind,
not inept, or so retarded,
it's only by the grace of God,
that we've not been discarded.

We take our life and then we shape
those things that we call dreams,
but those like Squeaky have no chance
with the hand they're dealt, it seems.

Like the birds and all things wild,
we share with them our things,
scattering crumbs of kindness
to creatures with smaller wings.

REFERENCES

Bloodworth, Venice (1952).
Key to yourself.
Marina del Ray,CA.

Bly, Robert (1988).
A Little Book on the Human Shadow.
New York, NY.

Bryson, Kelly MFT, (2002).
Don't Be Nice, Be Real.
Santa Rosa, CA.

Catford, Lorna Ph.D., and Ray, Michael Ph.D., (1991).
The Path of the Everyday Hero:
Drawing on the Power of Myth to Meet Life's Most Important Challenges.
Forrestville, CA.

Center for Disease Control and Prevention,
"Guillain-Barré Syndrome (GBS)," http://www.cdc.gov/flu/protect/vaccine/
guillainbarre.htm.

Eareckson-Tada, Joni (1976).
Joni.
Grand Rapids, Michigan

Epstein, Mark M.D., (2005).
Open to Desire: Embracing a Lust for Life.
New York, NY.

Frankl, Viktor E. (1984).
Man's Search for Meaning.
New York, NY.

Gobe, Marc (2001).
Emotional Branding: The New Paradigm for Connecting Brands to People.
New York, NY.

Goleman, Daniel (1995).
Emotional Intelligence: Why It Can Matter More Than IQ.
New York, NY.

Hamblin, Henry Thomas (1921).
Dynamic Thought
Yogi Publication Society

Hanh, Thich Nhat (1991).
Peace is Every Step: The Path of Mindfulness in Everyday Life.
New York, NY.

Healey, Terry (2006).
At Face Value.
Ashland, OR.

Hendricks, Gay Ph.D., & Hendricks, Cathlyn Ph.D., (1990).
Conscious Loving: The Journey to Co-Commitment.
New York, NY.

Keirsey, David and Bates, Marilyn (1978).
Please Understand Me: Character and Temperament Types.
Del Mar, CA.

Keyes, Ken Jr., (1981).
Prescriptions for Happiness.
Coosbay, OR.

Kushner, Rabbi Harold S. (1978).
When Bad Things Happen to Good People.
New York, NY.

Kushner, Rabbi Harold S. (1997).
How Good Do We Have to Be? A New Understanding of Guilt and Forgiveness.
New York, NY.

Levine, Steven (1982).
Who dies? An Investigation of Conscious Living and Conscious Dying.
New York, NY.

London, Peter (1989).
No More Secondhand Art: Awakening the artist within.
Boston, MA

May, Rollo (1975).
The Courage to Create.
New York, NY.

Miller, Alice (1994).
The Drama of the Gifted Child: The Search for the True Self.
New York, NY.

Miller, Alice (2006).
The Body Never Lies.
New York, NY.

Mitchell, Stephen (1988).
Tao Te Ching.
New York, NY.

Ray, Michael Ph.D (2004).
The Highest Goal: The Secret that Sustains You in Every Moment.
San Francisco, CA.

Ray, Veronica (1991).
Choosing Happiness: The Art of Living Unconditionally.
New York, NY.

Sarno, John E. M.D. (1998).
The Mindbody Prescription: Healing the Body, Healing the Pain.
New York, NY.

The Holy Bible:
Revised Standard Version.
San Francisco: Ignatius Press, 1966.

Welwood, John Ph.D, (1990)
Journey of the Heart.
New York, NY.

Yung, Judy (2007).
The Adventures of Eddie Fung.
Seattle, WA

Zukav, Gary (1990).
The Seat of the Soul.
New York, NY.

ABOUT THE AUTHOR.

A native of Santa Cruz, California, Ed Penniman graduated from the Chouinard Art School of California Institute of the Arts in Los Angeles in 1966 with a BFA. He has won design awards for corporate identity, packaging, and marketing communication design. In 1974 Communication Arts Magazine did a feature article about him. Examples of his design work have been published in the U.S., Europe and Japan. The American Institute of Graphic Arts (AIGA), celebrates achievement in book design "50 Books/50 Covers" and *Planet Steward: Journal of a Wildlife Sanctuary* by Steven Levine has been added to the AIGA Design Archives for one of the fifty best books designed of the year.

Ed is also an accomplished painter and his artistic journey has found him painting in many locations around the world. He has self-published a collection of poems titled *In Memoriam Innocentium* about love, loss, inspiration, healing, spirituality, hope and humor.

At age 42, Ed was stricken with Gullain-Barré syndrome (French polio), which left him a quadriplegic. In the years since he has come back physically (still disabled but no longer a quadriplegic), psychologically and spiritually to become a new and more functional person than before the trauma.